Your Questions Answered:

Narration

by Sonya Shafer

Excerpts from Charlotte Mason's books are surrounded by quotation marks and accompanied by a reference to which book in the series they came from.

Vol. 1: Home Education
Vol. 2: Parents and Children
Vol. 3: School Education
Vol. 4: Ourselves
Vol. 5: Formation of Character
Vol. 6: A Philosophy of Education

Your Questions Answered: Narration

Cover Design: John Shafer

ISBN 978-1-61634-281-4 printed
ISBN 978-1-61634-282-1 electronic download

Published by
Simply Charlotte Mason, LLC
930 New Hope Road #11-892
Lawrenceville, Georgia 30045
simplycharlottemason.com

Printed by PrintLogic, Inc.
Monroe, Georgia, USA

Contents

Chapter 1
Let's Talk about Narration

In my pantry are some foods I think of as staples. They can be included in a variety of dishes and used in a variety of ways. Take potatoes, for instance. I can add them to a stew or pop them in with a roast. I can bake them, boil them, mash them, slice them, shred them, fry them. I can serve them as a side dish or as the main dish with toppings for garnish.

Potatoes are a wonderfully versatile staple in my meals.

In a similar way, narration is a wonderfully versatile staple in my home school.

If you use the Charlotte Mason Method, narration is a staple. We use it in a variety of school subjects to help our students cement in their minds what they have learned. It's one of those can't do-without methods.

Narration can also be used in a variety of ways. It is a powerful learning tool that can be flexed and fitted to meet different needs in different situations at different levels.

In fact, I think that's one reason people have so many questions about narration. It might be easier to wrap our minds around it if it weren't quite so powerful and flexible.

Yes, narration can be simple—like making baked potatoes. I mean, how hard is it to put the potato in a hot oven and let it sit there for an hour?

But narration can also be much more multi-faceted and complex—like making *loaded twice-baked* potatoes. Same staple, but used in a different way to achieve a different outcome.

So let's talk about narration.

This book is a handy compilation of blog posts about narration that we have written over the years along with some added material. It's divided into three sections filled with helpful tips and practical how-to's.

The first section, Five Steps to Successful Narration, gives the big picture and shows you what a narration lesson looks like.

The second section, Narration Q & A, dives deeper into the specifics and answers questions submitted by homeschooling parents. You will also find some added Bonus Questions, narration samples, narration question samples, and more that we didn't have time or space to discuss in the blog posts. You will also see an index at the end of that section, listing all of the questions covered, so you can find the answers you need quickly and easily.

The third section gives More Narration Tips and advice from our archives about working with everyday situations and with special needs.

It is our hope that you will gain confidence and skill as we spend a little time talking about narration—that incredibly flexible staple in a Charlotte Mason home school!

Section 1
Five Steps to Successful Narration

Chapter 2
Five Steps to Successful Narration

My husband has been lifting weights for several months now in an effort to get into shape and improve his health. It's been good. The program he is using challenges him to regularly increase the number of pounds he lifts, and he was happily making progress and attaining new lift records until January rolled around. Then the wheels fell off the wagon.

All of a sudden he couldn't progress any farther. He couldn't lift anything heavier. What was wrong? After shooting some video and analyzing it, he discovered the problem: his form was off. He was not following the basic mechanics of how to lift correctly, and it was impeding his progress.

He had gotten to a certain level but he couldn't progress beyond that without correct form.

For those of us who use Charlotte Mason methods, it's good to examine our basic mechanics every once in a while too. I've talked to a lot of moms who are frustrated because they don't seem to be making any progress. They've reached a certain point and can't seem to get beyond it. When we discuss further, usually there is one component that they all mention. It's a basic component of Charlotte Mason that can either make or break your progress: narration.

If you are doing a narration lesson correctly, you will make great strides and your children will enjoy learning. If your form is off a bit, however, that deviation can hinder you from reaching your goals.

So let's go over the basics of narration—the correct form, if you will—that will help you continue to progress and experience success.

A Successful Narration Lesson

A successful narration lesson has five steps. Usually when a homeschool mom is frustrated with narration, it's because she is leaving out one of these steps.

1. Pick a good living book.
   Some books are well nigh impossible to narrate, even for an experienced narrator. If you're using one of those, you won't make much progress. You want to make sure the book you're reading touches the emotions, fires the imagination, and paints a picture that you can see in your mind's eye as the author describes what is happening. This type of living book—one that gives ideas, not just dry facts—will pave the way for a smooth narration lesson.

2. Look ahead and behind.
   This step is probably the one that is omitted most often. Yet it is an important part of the process and can make the difference between success and failure in a narration lesson. Take a few minutes to gain your bearings. Look at how today's reading connects to what happened last time and prepare your mind for what will be read about today.

3. Read the passage.
   Once your mind is prepared, let the author share his great ideas. Your mind will gain great food for thought. Just make sure that you know when to stop "eating," rather than continuing to stuff your mind too full and not allow time to digest. In other words, keep a watchful eye on the length of the passage you read.

4. Retell the passage.
   After the information comes into your mind, you must interact with it if you really want to know it. Considering what you read, pondering how it applies to other ideas you've gained, putting it into order, recalling details, mixing it with your opinion, and then forming those thoughts into coherent sentences and telling them to someone else is when real learning takes place. Charlotte Mason called this The Act of Knowing.

5. Discuss ideas.
   Any questions that are asked should be open-ended discussion questions that encourage more interaction with the author's great ideas. Questions such as these, and a lesson with all the components described above, will keep the focus on the joy of learning for personal growth. If you're encountering "Will this be on the test?" comments, that's a sure sign that something has shifted, your mechanics are off, and your progress is going to be hindered.

Let's take a little time to look at each step in more detail and get your narration lessons back into correct form.

Chapter 3
The Power of a Good Story

It's tempting to think that we can just open a book, start reading, ask one of the children to tell us what happened, and be done. But such a process leaves out a couple of key components that can make the difference between just going through the motions and real learning. And, after all, don't we want our efforts to result in real learning?

A narration lesson that results in real learning has five steps:

1. Pick a good living book.
2. Look ahead and behind.
3. Read the passage.
4. Retell the passage.
5. Discuss ideas.

Let's talk about Step 1: Pick a good living book.

The Power of a Good Story

I'm going to post two accounts here, both telling about the same event. Read both, then see what you think about the question that follows.

First, just the facts, ma'am.

> Sources report that an unnamed male was assaulted near the main highway. Several items in his possession are now missing. A male of mixed nationality found him and brought him to a local hotel to recover and has offered to reimburse any expenses incurred, according to the hotel manager.

Now the story form.

> A man was going down from Jerusalem to Jericho, and he fell among robbers, who stripped him and beat him and departed, leaving him half dead. Now by chance a priest was going down that road, and when he saw him he passed by on the other side. So likewise a Levite, when he came to the place and saw him, passed by on the other side. But a Samaritan, as he journeyed, came to where he was, and when he saw him, he had compassion. He went to him and bound up his wounds, pouring on oil and wine. Then he set him on his own animal and brought him to an inn and took care of

> him. And the next day he took out two denarii and gave them to the innkeeper, saying, "Take care of him, and whatever more you spend, I will repay you when I come back" (Luke 10:30–35, ESV).

So here's the first part of a two-part question: Which of the two accounts has the greatest potential to be remembered?

Most likely you will remember the story form best. The reason the story will stick in your head is because it touched your emotions and fired your imagination as you read. You were able to picture the action in your mind's eye—much more so than when you read just the facts—and that visual image will have lasting effects.

But there is something more. Yes, you will remember the story better and longer. Remembering is good; but remembering facts isn't going to educate in the true sense of the word. Only ideas can truly educate the whole person.

So here is the two-part question in full: Which of the two accounts has the greatest potential to not only be remembered but to shape you as a person?

Did you notice how the first account had been stripped of life lessons that educate us as people? There is a tiny glimmer in the easily-overlooked statement about reimbursement. But how many ideas are tucked into the second account? So many ideas that would have been especially poignant to the original audience: the positions of those who came by and how they reacted; the social status of a Samaritan and how he was viewed; having compassion on someone who probably despises you; getting your hands dirty and being inconvenienced to give first aid; using your own possessions to help someone you don't know; the amount of money and what that was worth in those days!

Now we have something to discuss in addition to simply remembering! Now we have a powerful tool for educating the whole person.

So all of that is to say that the very first step in having a successful narration lesson is to pick the right kind of book. The right kind of book, a good living book, will

- touch the emotions,
- fire the imagination,
- create mental pictures with its wording,
- and convey living ideas, not just dry facts.

Pick a good living book and narration will come easily.

Chapter 4
Find Your Bearings

Probably the best way to illustrate Step 2 is to talk about the importance of framework. I saw an interesting video clip in which some instructions were read that were difficult to remember or to relate with. But once the person gave the viewer one little phrase . . .

Whoa. Stop right there. Take a moment to analyze what your mind is doing. How are you feeling about this chapter?

Chances are you're either puzzled and floundering a bit or disengaged and skimming at this point. Why? Because I didn't help you find your bearings at the beginning.

Let's start over. Clear your mind; here we go. Ahem, . . .

I hope you've been finding this section on the 5 Steps to Successful Narration helpful. Remember that a good narration lesson has these five steps:

1. Pick a good living book.
2. Look ahead and behind.
3. Read the passage.
4. Retell the passage.
5. Discuss ideas.

In the last chapter we talked a bit about Step 1: Pick a good living book, and we used the story of the Good Samaritan as an example of what to look for. Do you recall anything about that story and the components it contained, which would make narrating easy?

Now let's talk a bit about Step 2: Look ahead and behind. This is a step that is often overlooked, but by now I hope you understand how important it is to help your reader or listener find her bearings as you get started.

Okay, stop again and analyze what you're thinking and feeling now. Do you feel a little more prepared to forge ahead? What made the difference? I guided you in looking behind and looking ahead. I helped you find your bearings—your position in relation to all the things you're dealing with.

When we jumped right into the details, with no hint of where we were in the discussion or where we were going, it was very difficult to focus and fully absorb what I was saying. But when we took just a minute to look behind and look ahead, your mind was better prepared to learn, because now it knew what to do with the input it was about to receive—where to file it, if you will.

Look Ahead and Behind

To help your reader or listener find her bearings, touch briefly on what was read last time from that book. Don't go into great detail, though; you want the student to do the mental exercise of pulling up that memory. Once that mental "rope" has been pulled out of the mental "well," it will be easy to tie the next portion of the book to it, thus constructing a continuous line of thought.

So encourage your student to remember the main points, or highlights, of last time's reading. Then give her a taste of what is coming in today's reading.

This step is also your opportunity to define any crucial words that you know will be needed for the student to understand. For example, I recently read a short story about *The Boy and the Filberts*. If I were going to read that story aloud to my children, I would want to tell them right up front that filberts are a type of hazelnut. Think about it. How can they picture the story in their mind's eye if they don't know what you're talking about?

Now, don't go overboard and give them a list of twenty vocabulary words from the chapter to look up and define before you read! Most words will be defined naturally in context. Don't steal the joy of a well-written story, but do give your students any crucial point that is necessary for understanding. Help them find their bearings.

One more hint. You may want to pull two or three key words from the reading for the day and write them on a little white board or sheet of paper so the student can see them. Use those words to help the student look ahead. Tell her that she will hear those three words in the story and should use those three words in her narration. Then leave the list on display while you read and while she narrates. Those words will gently guide her in learning to listen for key names or concepts, plus they will form little mental hooks for her narration. (And as an added bonus, she will see how those words are spelled.)

Looking behind is easy. It doesn't take any preparation to flip open the book, glance at the previous chapter, and say, "Oh, yes, last time we read about the Good Samaritan. What do you recall about that story?" But to help our students have a successful narration, we need to invest some time in preparing—in looking ahead, ourselves.

It will probably take less time than you expect, but we need to get in the habit of looking ahead before the lesson begins. Take a few minutes to look over the reading for today and find any key words or crucial points that will help your student find her bearings. Determine how today's reading can be tied to last time's reading.

That little extra time—to scout around the uncharted territory of the new chapter and determine how to help our students find their bearings as they take the next step—is an important part in successful narration. Try it this week.

Chapter 5
Time to Read

So far we've discussed the importance of selecting a good living book. Book selection can make or break your child's success at narration. We've also emphasized looking ahead and behind before you begin reading in order to help your child find his bearings and prepare his mind to absorb what you are about to share.

Unfortunately, in many parents' minds a narration lesson has only two steps: read and narrate. The end. But to have a successful narration lesson—one in which your child's mind embraces and enjoys living ideas on which to grow—you need all five steps:

1. Pick a good living book.
2. Look ahead and behind.
3. Read the passage.
4. Retell the passage.
5. Discuss ideas.

Now let's look at Step 3. It's time to read.

Read the Passage

The beauty of the Charlotte Mason method of using living books is that it relieves us of the burden of being the fountainhead of all knowledge. We do not have to bear the responsibility of telling our children everything they need to know about any subject at hand. We can let the great minds of great men and women do that. (And I daresay they will do a better job of it than we could.) All we have to do is read their ideas in the books we have selected. We can allow the book to be the teacher. It's a brilliant philosophy!

Our concern, then, is with the How: *how long* and *how often*. How long of a passage do we read? and How often do we read it?

How long we read depends somewhat on the student. If he is just starting out with this whole narration method, we read a short bit. If he is an old pro, we can read a longer portion. Aesop's fables are a great place to start with a beginner. They contain a whole story in just a paragraph or two. As the student gains experience and proficiency in listening and narrating, the length of the passage can be bumped out gradually until he is reading and narrating an entire chapter.

But don't get carried away. Even if a student can narrate a long passage, don't feel like you need to keep pushing the boundary. He will most likely benefit more from a moderate-length passage that he can ponder over than an epic-length passage that bombards him with too many ideas. When in doubt, too short is better than too long.

Now, for the second How—How often do we read the passage?—the answer is definite: once. We all have the very human tendency to not pay full attention if we know we can get another chance at hearing or reading the information. But such a tendency is the opposite of the habit of attention. And the habit of attention is the teacher's best friend. You will get a lot more accomplished, and have an enjoyable time doing it, if you cultivate the habit of full attention both within yourself and within your children. Reading the passage only once before requiring a careful narration can be a powerful motivator toward developing that habit!

This is another reason that we are careful not to read too long; the longer the passage, the harder it is to give it full attention. So be careful not to frustrate your students in their efforts to develop the habit of attention. Long passages, read once, are for those experienced and proficient in CM methods and habits. Shorter passages, read once, are your tool for getting there.

Chapter 6
To Narrate and Discuss

The time has come for your child to perform the Act of Knowing. We've discussed the first three steps to a successful narration lesson: pick a good living book, look ahead and behind, and read the passage. Those steps are foundational. Your narration lesson will be less than successful if you skimp on any of them.

But now it is time for the heart of the learning process: your child should retell the passage in his or her own words. Charlotte called this process the Act of Knowing, because you don't really know something until you actively ponder it and form mental connections with it and make it your own possession. In addition, telling someone what you now know cements it in your mind.

So narration provides a way to encourage the student to dig for his own knowledge, hold him accountable for doing so, plus secure that knowledge in his mind. It's quite the powerful method!

A few practical tips can make this retelling step flow smoothly. If you have several children together, let them take turns narrating portions of the passage. Make sure no one (not even you) interrupts the person who is narrating. If corrections or clarifications need to be made, wait until that person has finished his narration.

Older children who are experienced at narrating orally can write their narrations. Usually this gradual transition starts around fourth grade or so. Oral narration is a great way to practice organizing and communicating your thoughts. So make sure your children have plenty of practice doing that mental process before you add the extra challenge of putting it on paper.

Sometimes use a different approach to narration in order to keep things fresh. You might have the children draw their favorite scene or act out the story. Those who are writing their narrations could compose a diary entry from one character's point of view or take the challenge to write the narration in poetry form. There are all kinds of possibilities!

Discuss Ideas

If the passage lends itself to a short discussion, invite comments by posing an open-ended question after the narrations are done. Did you catch that? *After* the narrations have been given. You want to first give the children an opportunity to share what they noticed. If someone mentions the point you were going to bring up for discussion, all the better!

Encourage the children to talk about their opinions, to explain whether they would have chosen to do the same thing the main character did, to speculate what might happen as a result, to draw character traits from the attitudes and actions they read about. Don't feel like you must give three points and a poem or preach a sermon after every reading. Simply take advantage of the living ideas that will come naturally in a good book and draw attention to them with tact and kindness.

But watch yourself carefully. Yes, yourself. It will be all too easy to revert to the way you were probably taught by asking direct questions on the content. Don't do it. Asking direct questions on the content is the best way to squelch your child's natural curiosity for knowledge. The focus will quickly shift from learning for the joy of learning to Will this be on the test? Don't let that happen.

By providing your children with successful narration lessons, you will be equipping them to educate themselves for the rest of their lives. They will know how to perform the Act of Knowing and will be able to use that method for their own personal growth into adulthood.

Set your children up for success.

1. Pick a good living book.
2. Look ahead and behind.
3. Read the passage.
4. Retell the passage.
5. Discuss ideas.

Section 2
Narration Q & A

Chapter 7
The Why Behind the How

We just returned from a homeschool convention in Texas that required four days on the road and three days at the convention hall. You do the math.

During those days away from home, we ate in many different restaurants, and I noticed a trend among the informal ones. As we came in the door, an employee would call out, "Hello, welcome to [insert name of restaurant]!"

But I never felt welcome. You see, the employee never established eye contact, never smiled at us, never even identified herself. In fact, I often had to look around in confusion to see who might have hollered at us.

It's true that the employee was performing the required action—*greet everyone who comes in the door and say such-and-such*—but the purpose seemed to be lost. She knew what to do, but the Why behind it was missing; so her efforts ended up being an exercise in futility. Rather than feeling welcomed, I felt confused and a bit uneasy.

As we begin this Q & A on narration, I think we need to start with the Why behind the How. You see, we can spend lots of time discussing various techniques and how-to's until you feel confident in what to do, but if you don't fully grasp the *reason* Charlotte Mason used narration, your efforts may end up being an exercise in futility.

Why Narrate?

Many children wonder why we ask them to retell what was just read.

Narration Question #1: I always get the question from them, "Why do I have to tell it to you when you just read it?" I read everything to them right now.

It's a legitimate question. If the narration were for your benefit, as the teacher, telling you what you just read wouldn't make much sense.

But the truth is that the narration is for the *student's* benefit.

The mental work of narration—remembering, comprehending, organizing, sequencing, and forming into your own words—is a powerful tool! Information can enter your child's mind, but until that child works with it, processes it, and makes it his own, he doesn't really know it.

Narration helps the student make the material his own; it helps him cement the ideas and information in his mind. It helps the student know.

That's why Charlotte called this process "the act of knowing."

"They must read the given pages and tell what they have read, they must perform, that is, what we may call the act of knowing*" (Vol. 6, p. 99).*

To truly begin to understand the power of narration, you might want to try it for yourself. Take what you have read in this chapter about the reason we ask students to narrate, and (without looking back) put it into your own words so you can explain to your children the Why behind the How.

"Whatever a child or grown-up person can tell, that we may be sure he knows, and what he cannot tell, he does not know" (Vol. 6, pp. 172, 173).

Bonus Question: I understand that narration helps the student know, but are there any other reasons Charlotte chose to use the method?

Yes, Charlotte recognized several other Whys behind the scenes. You don't necessarily need to tell the student about these, but they are also wonderful benefits that come from using the method of narration.

1. Narration gives the student experience with composition. Every time you ask him to narrate—whether oral or written—he must go through the mental process of composition.

2. Narration encourages the student to rehearse the big picture in his mind. It's important to see the big picture and how the large pieces relate to each other before dissecting them into little bits and analyzing.

3. When a student knows he will be required to narrate after a single reading, he has motivation to pay attention!

4. Listening and narrating puts the responsibility for learning squarely on the student's shoulders. It prepares him to self-educate his entire life. And it makes the knowledge that he gains his prized possession, because he had to dig for it himself.

Chapter 8
In My Own Words

How well do you know The Pledge of Allegiance? I'm pretty sure most of us can recite it. Want to try? (Those of you residing in a country other than the United States, bear with me while I make a point.)

But how well do you know The Pledge of Allegiance? Try putting it in your own words.

No, don't just keep reading here. Stop and try to put The Pledge in your own words. Go ahead. I'll wait.

Did you do it? Now, here's the $10,000 question: Which of those exercises displayed true knowledge: reciting it or putting it in your own words?

Trying to put something in your own words requires much more of the mind and heart to be engaged. It is a higher-level thinking process than memorization and recitation. It requires you to interact with the ideas, process them, and understand them for yourself.

That's narration.

What is Narration?

Narration Question #2: What is narration exactly?

The short answer is that narration is retelling something in your own words.

It's interesting that we all turn to this technique quite naturally when we want to make sure we understand. We'll listen to someone who is telling us something, then we'll reply, "So what you're saying is . . . ," and we'll restate their message in our own words. It's a common tool to assure comprehension.

When we use narration—retelling something in your own words—for schoolwork, we are harnessing this powerful, yet natural, tool and teaching our children to use it intentionally to self-educate.

Which brings us to the next question.

Narration Question #3: How can I get my child to stop narrating word for word/ parroting passages? How can I encourage her to put it into her own words?

You might try asking her to draw a picture of the story, then explain her picture to you. She might act out the story. You could ask her to think of five questions covering the story and tell you the questions. (She has to know what was in the story to come up with the questions.) She could build her favorite part with interlocking blocks, then tell you about what she built.

Each of those variations will encourage your child to make the material her own—to process it and deal with it for herself—before she starts to talk. You'll find a list of narration variation ideas on page 25.

Bonus Question: Should I expect all of my children's narrations to be the same?

No, because your children are individual persons. It's fascinating that often our own personalities show through in what we say when we're narrating and how we say it. When my husband and I return home from traveling, we often tell the children about some of the experiences we encountered. They know that when Dad retells the story, he often can relate an exact facial expression or pick up on a particular phrase that brings out the humor of an event. My retellings are usually more along the lines of something I learned or a mental connection I made. We can be describing the same event, but our personalities will shine through in our words, emphases, and mannerisms.

It's the same with our children and narration. They may all read the same story written by the same author, but each one's narration will express some of his or her own individuality.

"Children shew the same surprising power of knowing, evinced by the one sure test,—they are able to 'tell' each work they have read not only with accuracy but with spirit and originality" (Vol. 6, p. 182).

Bonus Question: Why might my child be parroting from the book?

One common culprit can be the book itself. Check to make sure the book you are using is a living book—one that makes the subject "come alive"; one that allows the reader to picture in her imagination what is happening as she hears or reads for herself.

"Children cannot tell what they have not seen with the mind's eye, which we know as imagination, and they cannot see what is not told in their books with some vividness and some grasp of the subject" (Vol. 6, p. 227).

Narration Ideas

A key component of Charlotte Mason's method is narration. In simple terms, narration is telling back in your own words what you just read or heard. It's a wonderful evaluation tool that requires much thinking and assimilating on the student's part. Narration can be done in many ways; here is a list of suggestions.

Speaking

1. Compose and record a radio show that dramatizes the events read about.
2. Compare and contrast a practice in the account you read with a similar practice in modern society (for example, the feudal system vs. free enterprise; or infanticide in Rome vs. abortion today).
3. Compare and contrast two or three rulers read about who lived during the same time period or in the same country. Which one would you rather live under and why?
4. Play the part of the person you read about as he or she is being interviewed.
5. Explain what this story tells you about the character of the person you read about.
6. Name three things the person you read about is remembered for.
7. Tell all you know about . . . (for example, the habits of a bluejay or the founding of Rome).
8. Describe our . . . (for example, trip to the ocean or lighthouse experience).
9. Tell five things you learned from what you read.
10. Tell back the story in your own words.
11. Ask five questions covering the material you read.
12. (For Picture Study) Describe the picture you just saw.
13. (For Picture Study) Which picture did you like best of all you studied? Describe it.
14. Describe your favorite scene in the story you read.
15. Tell what happened into an audio recorder.
16. Tell how the scene reminds you of another story.
17. Say three questions you would ask if you were writing a test about what you just read.
18. Tell me anything new you learned from the passage.
19. Tell what may happen next and why.

20. Describe the problem and how it was solved or how it could be solved.
21. Tell what you think this means: "..."
22. Tell how you might have done things differently as a character.
23. Compare how people did things back in those days to how we do them today.
24. Describe any clues left by the author in previous readings pointing to the plot twist.
25. Describe a character's worldview. Compare it to a Christian worldview.
26. Compare kindred spirits from this book with those who might be good friends from another book.
27. Compare yourself to a kindred spirit of yours from this book.
28. Tell what you have learned about history, geography, or science from this book.
29. Describe any golden deeds from this book.

Writing

Any of the Speaking ideas listed above, done in written form, plus . . .

1. Write and perform a play that depicts the event read about.
2. Create a newspaper article about the event or person read. Put the article in a time-appropriate newspaper that you create; just the front page will do. Include ads, weather, and any other elements that would give the feel of the time period.
3. Write an obituary for a person you read about.
4. Write an interview with a person you read about.
5. Write journal or diary entries from the person's point of view whom you read about.
6. Write a letter to a younger sibling, explaining what you learned.
7. Write a poem that retells the story you read about.
8. Write five interview questions you'd like to ask the person you read about.
9. Write five questions covering the material you read.
10. Write five sentences about the passage.
11. Make a fill-in-the-blank quiz (oral or written) about the story for someone.
12. Write a letter (or e-mail) to someone about the passage.
13. Write a letter from one character to another.

14. Write a one-act play of a scene.
15. Write a letter from the author to the publisher about key scenes.
16. Write an imaginary conversation between two characters from two different books.
17. Write a review of the book for *amazon.com*.

Drawing

1. Draw a diagram of a machine or series of events you read about and explain it.
2. Draw a picture of the event or one particular scene in the event you read about.
3. Draw a map of the place you just read about.
4. (For Music Study) Draw a picture of what you hear in this composer's music.
5. (For Picture Study) Draw the basic components of this artist's work, putting each in its proper place.
6. Describe and/or draw a theme park based upon this book (adventure stories).

Drama

1. Write and perform a play that depicts the event read about.
2. Dramatize and video record a news broadcast that summarizes the events read about.
3. Spend 10 minutes planning a short skit based on what you read.
4. Describe how you would adapt the scene to a movie.
5. Describe special features for a DVD made from this book.

Building

1. Make a model of a machine you read about and explain how it works (for example, the Trojan horse or Archimedes' stone-throwing machine).
2. Set up the scene you just read about with blocks, toys, Legos, etc.
3. Model something from the scene with clay.

Chapter 9
The Simplest Way

I like simple.
Well, let me amend that statement.
I like simple as long as it's effective.
Now that we know what narration is, let's talk about how to use it.
Here's a simple description Charlotte gave for using narration effectively. This one statement can answer several of your questions.
Here's her statement:

"The simplest way of dealing with a paragraph or a chapter is to require the child to narrate its contents after a single attentive reading" (Vol. 3, p. 179).

A Paragraph or a Chapter

First, we should require the child to narrate "a paragraph or a chapter." Well, which is it?

Narration Question #4: Should we require narration of the entire passage/chapter/story read? Or, should we break it down into pieces if it's longer?

The answer is one that we all know and love: it depends. (Isn't that your favorite answer?) It depends on how experienced the student is at narrating. With beginners, you will need to start short and ask for a narration after a single paragraph.

As the student gains confidence and proficiency, you can start gradually nudging out the length of the reading before asking for a narration. If your student is doing well, try reading two or three paragraphs at a time and see how he does.

Be content to move slowly, securing the ground underneath your feet. Eventually you will be able to read an entire chapter before the narration is given, but don't sacrifice true knowledge on the altar of speed.

And a related question:

Narration Question #5: If we have a child who is supposed to be reading 10 pages but can't keep up with that much information to narrate, how do we handle narration?

You might want to check the book to make sure it is one that can be narrated easily. Some books just don't lend themselves well to narrating and should be culled from the reading list. If you are confident that the book is not the issue, try breaking the passage into shorter sections and working through it that way. You may not keep up with your originally-intended schedule, but which is more important: that you check off the book on a specific date or that your child really knows the ideas in that book and still enjoys learning? Keep your eyes on the real goal and teach the child.

After a Single Attentive Reading

The rest of Charlotte's simple statement addresses this question:

Narration Question #6: My question is that even though we have been doing narration for years, some of my kids will consistently automatically stop listening when I read to them and have no idea what the reading, book, story, etc. was even about. Lately I have been using audiobooks and even though they do the same thing, I replay them. I know this goes against CM habit training but we've tried the other way for years. I guess I'm asking if there's a reason I should NOT do this?

You're right, it's a habit issue. Habits are formed by repetition. The more often the children pay attention the first time the passage is read, the more that will become a habit. The more they don't listen until the second or third time the passage is read, the more that action will become a habit. It's all about which habit you want to cultivate. Your choice.

"This is a bad habit to get into; and we should do well to save our children by not giving them the vague expectation of second and third and tenth opportunities to do that which should have been done at first" (Vol. 3, pp. 179, 180).

Now, there are some tips and techniques you can use to encourage them to listen the first time, to help them be better prepared to narrate after a single attentive reading—in other words, to set them up for success. We'll share some of those ideas in the next chapter.

Bonus Question: How can I stop for a narration after every paragraph or two and still keep the lesson times short?

Charlotte Mason encouraged us to keep lessons short in order to help children cultivate that habit of full attention. She followed a schedule something like this:

- Grades 1–3: No lesson longer than 15–20 minutes (Many were shorter.)
- Grades 4–6: No lesson longer than 20–30 minutes
- Grades 7–9: No lesson longer than 30–45 minutes

So if you are starting out with a beginning narrator in, say, second grade, you would read a paragraph or two and stop for his narration. Then glance at the clock and see how much of the 15 minutes is left. If you have time, read another paragraph or two and ask for a narration. Glance at the clock. Go only as far as you can within the time limit.

Such a practice may seem slow going, but keep in mind that you are moving slowly on purpose in order to achieve two very important foundational goals. First, you are keeping the student's attitude toward narrating positive by not giving him more than he can chew. Second, you are cultivating the habit of attention by stopping the lesson before the student loses interest. He will get in the habit of paying attention for the whole lesson, and eventually, once that habit is solidly instilled, you will be nudging out the time to longer lessons.

Bonus Question: Do you have a recommendation for a book to use with beginning narrators?

Aesop's fables are a great place to start, because they contain an entire story in one or two paragraphs.

Chapter 10
Setting Them Up for Success

When I began using Charlotte Mason's method of narration, I thought it should look like this: We sit on the couch. I open the book and read the next chapter. I close the book and ask a student to retell the chapter in her own words. End of lesson.

But sometimes I would get blank stares. Sometimes the children had no clue what I had just read. Sometimes it took me half of the chapter to remember what had happened in the storyline last time and how this chapter fit into the overall scheme of things.

Something obviously wasn't working. So I did more research and found out that my mental picture of what a narration lesson should look like was woefully incomplete. That's when I discovered some tips and techniques from Charlotte that helped greatly!

Let's address some questions about what to do when we ask for a narration and all we hear is crickets chirping. How can we turn things around and set our students up for success?

Narration Tips and Techniques

Narration Question #7: What to do if the child cannot give a narration after a completed lesson, even after gentle prompts? Should the response to this situation vary with the age of the child or does it solely depend on the reason behind not being able to narrate the lesson?

There's the key phrase: "depend on the reason." The first two possible issues that we need to consider when a child cannot narrate are the book and the attention factor. Does the book lend itself easily to narrating? Try reading a chapter and narrating it for yourself to get a feel for it. If the book just isn't working well, find a different one. There are thousands of living books to choose from!

Also check the attention factor: Is my child unable to narrate because she wasn't paying attention to the reading? If that is the case, you know you have a habit issue on your hands. You may simply need to read a shorter passage and stop before you lose her attention.

If the book and the child's paying attention are not the problem, try some of the ideas we'll mention below.

Narration Question #8: We've been working on cultivating the habit of attention and best effort over the past couple months. Sometimes when I ask my child to tell back what she remembers after a brief reading she says she doesn't know what to say, but I know she listened. What do I do when she's reluctant to narrate after a first reading?

Sometimes beginning narrators aren't quite sure what they're supposed to say. After all, they've probably never used this method before, nor heard anyone else use it. You may want to do a couple of narrations yourself to model for the student what you are expecting from her.

And when you finish your narration, be sure to invite your student to add or clarify anything she would like to. Sometimes students freeze when they think we (or they) are expecting perfection. Try to demonstrate what it looks like to give your best effort while also acknowledging that others can contribute some things that you might have left out, and that's okay.

Narration Question #9: How do I encourage a younger child who consistently responds, "I don't know"?

If you've ruled out the not-paying-attention possibility, it may be that the child was lost during the reading. Think about what it's like when you come in in the middle of a conversation and don't know what is being discussed. Sometimes we can leave our students floundering, lost at sea, when we just pick up in the middle of a book and take off reading.

Before you launch into reading the passage for the day, take a moment or two to recall what happened in that book last time. You don't have to require a detailed complete narration again, but help your student remember enough about last time's reading to remind him of the framework and know where today's chapter fits in that framework.

Narration Question #10: My 13-year-old seems to freeze when I say, "Tell me about…". I really think she doesn't listen well—probably more visual like me. Any advice?

After you've done the pre-reading review described above, you'll want to briefly whet the student's appetite for today's reading. Build anticipation about what she will hear or read. Sometimes it helps to include a visual in those introductory remarks.

Another possibility might be that she can process better if she sees the words for herself. You might allow her to sit beside you and look at the book as you read aloud, or give her another copy and let her follow along as you read, or she may be ready to do more silent reading on her own.

Narration Question #11: I'm trying to get started with narration with my six-year-old. She says "I don't remember" when I ask what the story was about. Do I ask leading questions to get her started?

We want to be cautious about cultivating a dependence on hints and prompting. Try this idea instead. Before the reading, take a couple of minutes to look over the passage for today and pull out two or three key words. Write those words on a small white board or a sheet of paper. During your introductory remarks, show those words to your student and briefly go over them. Tell her that you want her to especially listen for those words during the reading and be sure to include them in her narration. Then leave the list in sight as you read and as she narrates.

Narration Question #12: How do I motivate my child when she just doesn't "feel" like narrating?

First we try to make the path as smooth as possible for her with the ideas outlined above. If those techniques don't help, it may be that you have a character issue on your hands. You might tell her that you don't "feel" like making supper that night or doing her laundry that week or . . . you get the idea. Part of growing up is growing strong enough to make yourself do things even when you don't feel like doing them; that's a lesson many of us wrestle with our entire lives. This may be a prime opportunity to encourage her in strengthening her will so she will be able to do what she knows she should no matter how she feels.

It might also help to make sure your child knows why she is being asked to narrate. Share with her how she can use the process to help herself learn. (See chapter 7.)

Isn't it great how narration gives us opportunities to set our children up for success in their schoolwork, as well as in life? I hope these tips are helpful to you in that process!

Bonus Question: How can I learn more about this process of setting my child up for success in a narration lesson?

Make sure you read the first section in this book, Five Steps to Successful Narration.

Chapter 11
The Long and Short of It

I was listening to a music teacher talk about Chopin yesterday. He mentioned that some people might think Chopin was a lesser composer than Beethoven because Chopin's compositions are so much shorter.

But the music teacher set everyone's doubts to rest on that matter. Chopin's works might be shorter, but they are just as well-planned, just as intricately crafted, and just as difficult to perform as Beethoven's longer epic pieces.

That comment got me thinking about narration. Sometimes we get caught up in the length of the narration. Especially if you are just starting out with this tool of education, knowing what to expect in this area can be very helpful. So we're going to address a few questions on the length of narrations. But as we do, let's reflect on this timely reminder that—long or short—the most important factor for a composition is its quality.

The Length of Narrations

Narration Question #13: How long should a narration be (on average)?

The length of a narration usually depends on the length of the reading. It should be long enough to cover the material that was read. A narration on a paragraph will most likely be shorter than a narration on a full chapter.

Narration Question #14: How much narration is "enough"? My 9-year-old only says about 2 sentences every time no matter the length of reading.

The length will vary, but it helps to keep in mind the *purpose* of the narration. It's like saying, "How much baking time is enough for a cake?" We're not looking at the time so much as the goal: when it is done, we will pull it out of the oven to eat. Whether it took 25 minutes or 35 minutes isn't the point. The point is that the cake has finished baking. Just so, the length of the narration can vary, but the purpose is what you want to focus on. What you are looking for is to see the student go through the process of cementing the material into his mind.

Narration Question #15: What about narrations that seem to take as long as the reading itself?

You may want to take up knitting. I say that in half jest, half seriousness. Sometimes we get impatient when a student takes longer than we expected or scheduled. Especially if the student is just starting out with narration, she may require some extra time for this higher level thinking skill. We certainly don't want to short circuit her efforts at learning to self-educate, so try not to rush a student who is genuinely engaged and doing her best. She will improve with practice. With knitting, you can give her your attention and at the same time keep your hands busy and feel productive.

But if the student seems to be all at sea and floundering in a flood of words, you might throw her a lifeline by asking her to narrate in a different way. Some alternate narration ideas can give her a little more guidance than "tell all you know" and help her move through the material mentally; for example, you might ask her to make up half a dozen questions that cover the content or draw a picture of her favorite scene and tell about her picture. You'll find a list of alternate ideas on page 25.

Narration Question #16: What to do with a child (almost 9) who can narrate about the full text literally? (About as long as I read, even with long pieces of texts). We're only just beginning to homeschool, so he needs guidance to know what is most important and to be brief. How do I direct him in that?

We want to be careful about parroting. A child who simply repeats to you what you read—no matter the length—is not making the material his own. Charlotte said that "narrations which are mere feats of memory are quite valueless" (Vol. 1, p. 289). So you may want to use some of the alternate narration ideas from page 25 to help him see that there is more than one way to deal with the material. You may want to list some key words on the board and tell him to use those words in his narration or perhaps take some turns at narrating, yourself, to give him a model of what you expect. I would also recommend, since you are just beginning, to be sure you are using short passages. He may be reciting long passages because there is just so much material to deal with in his mind.

Narration Question #17: What do you do with children who are resistant to narrating? We are fairly new to narrating, and my 2 oldest children, ages 9 and 7, balk, complain and get irritated when I ask them to narrate back to me. I try to ask some leading questions, and they give the shortest answers possible. Or, they'll tell a one-line narration of what we just read, instead of telling the story back in their own words.

Keep in mind that, if they are new to narration and have been doing fill-in-the-blank questions in the past, you are now asking them to master a harder skill than they are used to. So grace and patience will be helpful. Make sure the book is interesting. Make sure you are reading short passages. Be cautious of asking leading questions; the students may just need more time to organize their thoughts when they are pausing. You might also want to try some of the alternate narration ideas on page 25, like drawing or building favorite scenes and then telling about them.

I would also urge you to be careful of inadvertently allowing the students to slip into a habit of complaining. The work may require more effort than they want to give, but complaining need not be allowed. In fact, the more times they are allowed to complain, the more that habit will become ingrained. So I would encourage you to let them know that complaining is no longer allowed. Complaining will bring immediate consequences. Effort toward this new way of learning will be expected and encouraged. Let them know why they are narrating, then lead the way toward self-education with confidence.

Chapter 12
Correct Me If I'm Wrong

So far we've talked about the reason we use Charlotte Mason's method of narration and how it cements the material in the student's mind; we've discussed what narration is and how to get started with it, how long of a passage to read and how many times to read it; we've looked at techniques we can use to set our students up for success in their narration lessons and considered how long or short their narrations should be.

But we all know that no matter how great the book is or how carefully we pave the way for a good narration, sometimes mistakes are going to happen. We and our children are human. Maybe your daughter isn't feeling well and she leaves out a key point. Or maybe your son stayed up too late the night before and his brain is having a hard time getting going and he mixes everything up in his narration. How do we handle situations like those?

In this chapter let's take a look at what to do with mistakes and omissions.

Handling Mistakes and Omissions

Narration Question #18: What do I do if my child narrates back with incorrect information, especially on something like a Bible narration?

As a teacher, our role is to be a guide. Part of a guide's job is to make sure you're heading the right direction. If you took the wrong path and the guide didn't say anything, he wouldn't be a very good guide.

We may need to correct a student's narration mistake at times. Charlotte gave specific direction for that situation:

"Corrections must not be made during the act of narration, nor must any interruption be allowed" (Vol. 6, p. 191).

So, yes, correct any incorrect points when necessary, but wait until the end of the narration. Don't interrupt.

Narration Question #19: What do I do if my child is narrating things out of order?

Often beginning narrators struggle with remembering the sequence of events. They may need some guidance to help them get into the habit of narrating in order. I once saw a video of a masterful Charlotte Mason-trained teacher demonstrate how to gently guide the narration to be given in order, yet she didn't stifle the students or overly direct them. She simply helped them focus on the various aspects of the passage in the correct order. It was almost like moving a spotlight to the different segments of the story to highlight the order.

You could follow her example by reading the passage, then saying something like, "Let's start with the first thing that happened and go from there. First, so-and-so arrived at such-and-such. Tell me about that." Allow the child to tell what he remembers about that part, then direct his attention to what happened next: "Good. After that, so-and-so did such-and-such. What do you recall about that?" And continue in that manner, guiding the student through the chain of events in order. As he gains more practice, you might ask him to move the mental spotlight for himself occasionally, "And what happened next after that?," to see how he is progressing in this skill of retelling in order. Keep gently guiding the sequencing process until it becomes a habit.

Narration Question #20: How to encourage more indepth/detailed narration without "digging it out of them"? We've been narrating for 4 years now and I don't feel like I am getting good narrations from them. I get "She went to that place and saw him." I can get a sentence or two out of a reading. I know that they know more than that.

It sounds like you may be dealing with a habit of carelessness. I would recommend you take steps to reestablish the good habit of doing a thorough job. Here are some practical tips. During a neutral time (not directly at the end of one of their abbreviated narrations) have a short talk. Something as simple as, "I expect your narrations to be more thorough. When you retell something it helps to cement it in your own mind. So from now on, I want you to work hard at remembering and retelling what we read."

During the next narration lesson, if you get the usual cryptic response, give them a firm yet pleasant look as you say, "I'm sure you know more than that." Then be prepared to sit quietly, with an expectant and encouraging look on your face, until they give you more. It may help to use the key-words-on-the-board technique (explained in the answer to Narration Question #11 given in chapter 10), offering them practical assistance as they put forth the effort to form the habit of thoroughness. As with other habits, you may also need to use the motivation of natural consequences. You could schedule the narration lesson immediately before an event they enjoy very much. If you have to spend too much time waiting for a thorough narration, they miss the enjoyable event.

The main point is that the more often they give you a meaningless narration, the more that will become a habit. You want to motivate them to form a habit of thoroughness instead.

Narration Question #21: What do I do if my child leaves out a key point in a narration?

This situation sounds more like a once-in-a-while inadvertent omission, rather than a habit. In that case, you might chime in with a narration of your own and include the student's omitted point in yours. Or you might bring up that point in a discussion question. Discussion questions are great tools to use after the narration.

We'll talk more about discussion questions—when to use them, how to word them, and what their purpose is—in the next chapter.

Bonus Question: Why did Charlotte say not to interrupt a narration?

Think about the last time you started to tell something to one person and had someone else interrupt with a question or a comment. That interruption can really derail your train of thought! You listen to the second person, then turn back to the first person to continue your conversation, and you have to take a moment to try to remember what you were talking about and where you left off and what you were going to say. So many thoughts that were lined up to flow out of your mouth have now disappeared because of the interruption.

Or maybe this has happened to you: You started to tell a friend something and she jumped in and finished your sentence, only she didn't finish it correctly. So you backtracked and tried again to convey what you were thinking, and she interrupted you again in the next sentence to put words in your mouth that were not your own. How frustrating to feel like you are not being heard!

Because the child is a person—and deserves the respect due to a person of value—we are careful not to allow others to interrupt his train of thought or to jump in and try to finish his sentences for him. (Sometimes this is hardest for Mom!)

Narrating is difficult enough without added distractions like interruptions. Let's do all we can to protect that time for each student and use it to affirm the respect due to a person when he is sharing his ideas and thoughts.

Chapter 13
The Next Step

It's easy to look at narration as the be-all and end-all Charlotte Mason method of learning. What we don't realize is that we are focusing on just a portion of the picture; we mistakenly think that a CM-style lesson is, *They read. They narrate. That's it.*

Narration is a powerful tool, but it is not complete all by itself. There are other steps that come before and after a narration that paint the rest of the picture and help our children learn well.

We already talked about doing a pre-reading review and a brief introduction to help our children mentally prepare for the passage about to be read. (See chapter 4.)

Then we read the passage and ask for a narration of it.

The next step is just as important: the discussion. The discussion is a great time to encourage students to expand on their narrations, to clarify certain points, or to summarize and organize what has been narrated.

Narration Question #22: How to get the children to expand on their narration? Or do you just accept whatever they narrate, because it is "theirs"?

We do want the children to form their own relations, but as their guide, it is perfectly acceptable to point out things they may not have seen along the way and to encourage them to think more deeply or broadly. A discussion after the narration is a prime opportunity to do that.

Now, we need to be careful of misusing the discussion time. Sometimes it's tempting to fire off a series of direct questions on the content of what was read, quizzing the student to see if he knows the parts he didn't mention in his narration.

Charlotte said, "Direct questions on the subject-matter of what a child has read are always a mistake" (Vol. 1, p. 228).

Narration Question #23: What's the difference between a narration question and a direct question on the content?

A direct question on the content can usually be answered with one or two words or a short phrase directly from the passage; whereas, a narration-style discussion question presents a topic and invites the student to tell what he knows and thinks about it.

It would be the difference between "Who won the race: the tortoise or the hare?" versus "What do you recall about the end of the race? Why, do you think, did it end that way?"

Narration Question #24: Why did Charlotte say that direct questions are a mistake?

Charlotte often talked about the idea that when a person is truly self-educating, he will pose questions to himself about the passage and try to answer them. When the teacher poses the questions, that changes the entire focus. Now it is no longer self-education—learning for myself so I can grow personally—but a performance-based mind-set—guessing what the teacher will ask and having the answer she wants.

Most of us were "educated" with the direct-questions method. Many of us learned how to jump through those hoops and perform well enough to get good grades. But how much of that material do we really know?

And so we happily use something different with our students: narration and discussion.

Narration Question #25: Mason writes in Vol. 1, p. 233: "When the narration is over, there should be a little talk in which moral points are brought out, pictures shown to illustrate the lesson, or diagrams drawn on the blackboard." I'd like to know how we are to do this without encroaching upon the student's understanding of the text. How are we to bring out the moral points? I'm particularly interested in this as it pertains to literature and Bible.

The discussion can highlight certain aspects of the passage that was read in order to expand on a point, clarify a portion, summarize main points, or organize what the student learned from it.

For example, in a lesson on Alexander the Great, the teacher would invite the students to discuss some character traits observed in the reading for the day. She had certain character traits in mind to suggest if the students did not bring them up. You can do the same with literary or Biblical characters: inviting the students to share what they think and to support their observations as appropriate, sharing what you think, and pointing out omissions or misunderstandings with care.

Pictures of artifacts or people can be used to illustrate or help students relate with something that was mentioned in the story, much like *The Stuff They Left Behind* portfolios do (available at simplycharlottemason.com). Maps and diagrams can also be used to clarify or elaborate on something that was read about in the passage.

The main point is to make sure the book remains the source of knowledge; the teacher merely helps the student organize the knowledge that he gained from the book.

"The teachers give the uplift of their sympathy in the work and where necessary elucidate, sum up or enlarge, but the actual work is done by the scholars" (Vol. 6, p. 241).

Bonus Question: What kinds of "moral points" should we bring out in discussion questions?

Charlotte urged teachers to be very careful to emphasize principles, not personal opinions. We need to teach our children to think through changing circumstances and relationships based on unchanging truth. Emphasizing principles would mean, for example, the difference between asking the student to "Explain why you should never eat store-bought bread" versus "Explain what constitutes healthful food," or the difference between "What should every fourth grader know?" versus "How can you tell if a student is making progress in his education?"

Giving children only personal opinions does not equip them to think things through for themselves. This does not mean that you should never voice your own opinions; rather, you need to be careful to point children to the solid principles behind your opinions and show them how you based your opinions on them. Use discussion questions to teach them how to think, not only what to think; for times change, and they will face situations that we never dreamed of. It is the unchanging principles that will give them a firm foundation on which to build future solid and just opinions.

And if I may add one more idea here, be watchful of the "unwritten curriculum" that your discussion times can convey to your children. The way in which discussions are carried out will greatly influence their communication skills and how they will treat others during future conversations. Be careful to show each person respect. Listen to understand, not just to reply.

Chapter 14
In Which We Talk More about When and How

I love this comment that Megan shared on our blog: "I did my first oral narration with my 9 year old son today after watching (and being SO encouraged) by the *Learning and Living* DVD set. He did pretty well, but most importantly, he enjoyed it and twenty minutes later came up to me and said, 'the stuff I told back to you is stuck in my head!' "

What an encouragement that narration really does work!

Let's address a few questions on when narration should be done and take another look at the big picture.

When to Narrate

Narration Question #26: Should narration be done immediately after a reading, or later in the day?

In Charlotte's descriptions and sample lessons, the teacher requested the narration immediately after the book was read. (And by the way, the time limit that Charlotte mentioned for a lesson like that included the time for the narration. So if you have a 20-minute history lesson, that time limit should include both the reading and the narration.)

So yes, narration should be done immediately after the reading, but not *only* immediately after the reading. Read on.

Narration Question #27: Does narration include asking questions to refresh memory when you continue reading a book another day?

Yes, part of the preparation for a new reading is to help students recall what happened last time that book was read. This pre-reading review does not need to be as thorough or as long as the one that is given immediately after a reading, but it should recall enough to help the student find his bearings and realize how the next part of the book relates to the previous one.

Be sure to word the pre-reading review questions as narration prompts and not as direct questions on the content. I've found it helpful to say something like, "Last time we read about how Benjamin West kept clipping fur from his cat. What do you remember about that?" or "Last time we read about how Benjamin West needed hair to make his paintbrushes. What do you remember about that chapter?"

Charlotte also asked students for long-term narrations. At the end of every term (12 weeks), she would have exams. The exam questions were narration questions over the books that had been read.

So the students used narration immediately after a reading, before the next reading in that book, and at the end of the term.

The Big Picture

Narration Question #28: I'm discouraged with narration and my 9-year-old. I'm using a classical education textbook and the sample narrations it gives don't resemble what my daughter narrates back to me. Hers are far less perfect. I am wondering how structured you think narration instructions should be? Is it too structured to ask a 9-year-old to narrate the story in no more than three sentences—and in one go? We often have to do a "rough draft" narration first, and then revise (as they are written narrations). I worry that the frustration is building and possibly spoiling a love for writing, no matter how patient I am with trying to help her develop her narration skills.

I think your instinct is guiding you rightly. Especially in the first few years, narrations should be oral and should allow the student plenty of leeway to deal with the big picture. Written analysis, in a Charlotte Mason approach, is not introduced until the student has had years and years of experience freely dealing with the larger ideas and concepts.

Summaries require a lot of analytical thinking in parts; but good analytical thinking in parts requires a lot of understanding of the whole. Give your daughter the freedom to look at the whole picture for several more years and tell you what she sees there. Celebrate and affirm what she knows rather than forcing her to pick it apart and present it as a mandatory dissected tidbit. You will reduce the frustration level and restore her joy in learning.

Bonus Question: Why did Charlotte do the pre-reading reviews?

Charlotte likened the pre-reading reviews to pulling up the bucket from the well of the student's mind and tying the next part of the narrative onto that rope to make one continuous string of thought. With all of those ideas tied to each other, any reference to one part of the story will mentally stay connected to the other parts and bring to mind the whole thing.

Chapter 15
Magic Numbers

- Eat three square meals a day.
- Brush your teeth twice a day.
- Change the oil every 3,000 miles.
- Take the trash to the curb once a week.

Many of us love guidelines with numbers, because it's easier to wrap our heads around the information that way. It helps us get a mental picture of what we should expect.

But even guidelines with numbers are open to debate. Maybe your health is such that you can't eat a lot of food at one sitting. Maybe you are using a different kind of oil that works longer. Maybe you take your own trash to the dump.

It is the principles behind the numbers that are most important. The numbers may change, but the principles remain constant.

- Eat healthful food at regular intervals throughout the day to keep a steady supply of energy.
- Clean your teeth often to remove food particles that can cause pain and decay.
- Change the oil in your vehicle frequently to help keep your engine clean and running smoothly.
- Remove trash from your house to avoid a stockpile of smelly garbage.

The principles behind the numbers are important to keep in mind when we talk about narration too. In this chapter we will address some questions about the frequency of narrating. I may give some number suggestions, but make sure you keep your focus on the principles behind those numbers and use the tool of narration as it best fits your child and your family situation.

The Frequency of Narrations

Narration Question #29: Do we require narrations of all books/subjects after age six? I seem to remember reading somewhere that certain subjects are just for enjoyment and they do not narrate them, but I cannot remember where I read that, or if it is true.

You are correct that narrations should not be required of a child younger than six. You probably read that here:

"Until he is six, let Bobbie narrate only when and what he has a mind to. He must not be called upon to tell *anything" (Vol. 1, p. 231).*

As to which subjects, keep in mind that Charlotte Mason did not use the read-a-living-book-and-narrate-it method for all school subjects. That method was used primarily for history, geography, Bible, science, and literature. So those five subjects will be your main focus.

Narration Question #30: Should I make my kids narrate everything they (and I) read?

This is where it is vital to keep in mind the purpose of narration: we ask the student to narrate in order to cement the material in his mind. So a guideline that can help with this question is to ask yourself *How important is this material? Do I want my student to put forth the effort to purposely remember it?* If the answer is Yes, require a narration.

But you might answer No sometimes. One possible scenario for answering No might be historical fiction books. I like to use that genre to give my students a good "feel" for the time period, but it is not important that they cement in their minds the invented story. So I might not ask for a narration on that particular book.

You decide how to use the tool of narration based on what you want to accomplish.

Narration Question #31: Should I vary the subjects daily in which narration is expected (for example: Monday-History, Tuesday-Literature, etc.) OR should I consistently have my children narrate from the same subject(s) each day, as in a written history narration is required after every history reading, etc.?

The answer to this question also depends on what you want to accomplish. If you have determined that you want the material from the history book to be cemented in your student's mind, then ask for a narration every time it is read.

Variety, however, is a good thing. Narrating every day is not an issue; narrating from the same book every day will quickly grow stale. Charlotte was careful to arrange her weekly schedule to do different subjects (with different books) on different days.

Depending on the age of child, you could add variety by sometimes requiring an oral narration, sometimes requiring a written narration, or using some of the alternate narration ideas on page 25.

Narration Question #32: How many narrations should I require daily? Oral? Written? Both?

It's interesting to look at Charlotte's schedules and see how many read-a-living-book-and-narrate-it subjects she covered during a given day. In grades 1–3, it was often only one, sometimes two subjects per day; grades 4–6, it was two, sometimes three per day; for the upper grades, it was usually three. So, based on her schedule, we can assume that's how often she required narrations daily.

Whether those narrations are oral or written depends on the level of the child. Charlotte asked for oral narrations in all the grades; around grade 4 she began to ask for some of the narrations to be written.

Here are some suggestions for what that might look like. If your 4th grader is reading and narrating two, sometimes three, books per day, you would probably want most of those to remain oral narrations; you might ask for one written narration per week in order to gradually phase them in. As your student gets more comfortable putting his thoughts on paper, you could gradually increase the number of written narrations required until, in high school, he would probably be writing at least one or two narrations every day.

But that's just one suggestion of what it could look like. As always, teach the child and keep the principles behind the numbers in mind.

Bonus Question: How important is it to follow the grade level suggestions for narration requirements?

Grade levels can be a blessing and a curse. They can help us get a handle on where a student is in the process, but they can also handcuff us and our children if we're not careful. When it comes to narration (or any school subject, for that matter) grade level suggestions are just that: suggestions. They are not chiseled in stone. They should never dictate what we will teach or what we should expect of a child. Each child is an individual, not a grade number. Grade levels do not take into account the very individual-ness of your child.

Use grade level suggestions as a starting point or a broad guideline, but remember that it is more important to give your child what he needs to take the next step from where he is now—whether that aligns with a particular grade level or not. Encourage, challenge, motivate, but don't frustrate, don't panic, don't push.

Look at the suggestion and look at where your child currently is. If the suggestion is a natural next step, fine. If it is seven giant steps away from where he is right now, keep that goal in mind so you know where you're headed but don't try to make that jump all at once. Wait until the child is ready.

Chapter 16
Narration with Multiple Children

When we think of narration, we often envision a parent and a child sitting comfortably on the couch. The parent is smiling and nodding—the book closed and resting in her lap—as the child earnestly tells the story in his own words.

But what does it look like with two children? or four? or fifteen?

As we continue answering narration questions, let's address narration with multiple children.

First off, let's settle one thing in our minds: Charlotte Mason used narration with multiple children. She trained her teachers to use the method of narration in a classroom full of students. So, fear not; narration can and does work with multiple children.

Here are some practical ideas and suggestions for using narration with multiple children in your home school. There are several ways you can approach it, and I would suggest that you use all of them at various times to keep things fresh.

Narration Question #33: How do you do narration with multiple children? Does the youngest go first?

That's one way to approach it, yes. You can start with the youngest and have him narrate everything he can remember. Then you can go down the row of children in age order and ask each one, "Do you have anything to add?"

I don't recommend that you use this approach exclusively, or even often, for the older ones catch on very quickly. Soon you may hear a chorus of, "No, nothing to add; he did a great job!" Keep this technique as just one of many narration possibilities.

Narration Question #34: I have a 6th, 4th, and 3rd grader and sometimes it's a little tricky to make sure the first child doesn't narrate everything. I know it's been recommended to start with the youngest, then work your way up, but by the time the two younger students narrate, my oldest has been sitting there for 10 minutes before she has anything to add (if there is anything left).

Another way to approach narration with multiple children is to start with the youngest and then *require* each child after that to add something that has not already been mentioned. If you run out of content before the final student's turn, don't panic; that is a prime opportunity for older children (approximately 10 and older) to do more with the material than simply retell. They might explain how a particular object in the story worked. They might give a comparison and contrast of what was read with something else in a different book, or they might offer an opinion on one of the character's personal traits. They might explain how and why a character in this story reminds them of a certain character in another story. This is their opportunity to branch out into critical thinking skills.

But also keep in mind that you don't have to start with the youngest every time. You can simply select any child to give a full narration, then open it up for corrections or additions from any of the others. Since the children don't know who will be called on to go first, they will all benefit from that heightened sense of attention that comes along with knowing you must be prepared to narrate.

Narration Question #35: If I do a read-aloud, should all of my children narrate (one after the other)?

I would probably not have each child give a full narration of the entire passage, one after another. Such repetition would be tedious. But you can involve all of them by doing a more guided, collaborative-style narration. Here's how.

Select a child to start telling. At some point in the narration, stop that child and have him choose who should pick up the story from there. The newly selected child should continue the narration until you stop him and he chooses who is next, and so on. You can even use a visual object with this technique if you would like to. Use a ball or a beanbag or a flower or a microphone (if you dare) and simply pass it to the person whose turn it is to narrate. No one is allowed to speak except the one holding the object.

Narration Question #36: How do you handle narration with multiple children at once? Or is it something you work on with children individually?

We do want to encourage the children to use the method of narration as a means toward self-education. It is a wonderful method that can help anyone learn, even in the adult years. (Try it yourself sometime.) As the children get older, they will make the transition to more written narrations. So you might read the book aloud to everyone, then dismiss the older students to go write their narrations in another room while you listen to oral narrations from the younger ones.

Narration Question #37: With many children to homeschool from 17 to 6, how do I incorporate narration? Daily with each? Different types? Some are working by themselves and others as a group with me. I just get overwhelmed with the idea and feel like it'll take a lot of time, so I don't do it much although I really want to.

As we discussed in chapter 15, the frequency of narrations can change as the students grow. As they get older, they should do more of their narrations in writing. So your teens who are working by themselves can simply be assigned a written narration on what they read independently. If you want to require an oral narration instead, give them an audio recorder of some kind (You may already have one around on a smartphone, iPod, or other device.) and have them record their narrations when they are ready. That way they won't have to wait for you to be available. You can read their written narrations or listen to their recorded narrations later (when you are finished with the youngers) and give them feedback or bring up any discussion points.

That leaves only the younger ones to deal with as a group, using the ideas outlined above. I think you will be pleasantly surprised at how little time narration actually takes and how large of a dividend it pays!

Bonus Question: I know that narration helps cement the material in my student's mind, but are there any other benefits to doing narration?

Absolutely, yes! Charlotte believed that oral narration provided a great introduction to public speaking. The student learns to gather his thoughts, organize them, and present them orally. As he progresses through the grades, he is challenged to ponder and present more and more complex speeches as oral narrations.

Written narration holds additional benefits too. It provides an opportunity for the student to demonstrate what he does know, rather than emphasizing what he doesn't; so it encourages personal growth and loving knowledge for knowledge's sake. It also gives the student a brilliant process through which to learn and refine his writing skills and voice.

And possibly the best part of using narration as a learning tool is that it equips the student to self-educate. Once the habit is set up—a habit of reading with full attention and then mentally pondering, reviewing, and dealing with the material for himself—the student can continue to learn for the rest of his life.

Chapter 17
Beginning with Younger Children

In the chapters so far, we have covered most of the foundation. The tips and techniques that we have discussed apply to most age ranges and give the broad view of narration.

In the rest of this section, we will focus on how this powerful tool can be tweaked and adapted to be most effective at specific stages of a student's educational journey. So let's start at the beginning.

My third daughter graduated this year. As I was reading her final high school narration, my mind wandered back to when she was just beginning formal lessons at home. Her big eyes would peer at me out of her sweet little face as she listened carefully to the book I was reading aloud; and her blond hair would bounce as she bobbed her head in time to her words when she was narrating.

It's a special time when a little one is first introduced to Charlotte Mason's wonderful method of narration. Here are some questions and answers about getting started with younger children.

> **Narration Question #38: In the *Learning and Living* DVD series you mention that narration should not be required of a child younger than six, if I remember correctly, including an example of not trying to do so "secretly" when daddy comes home. What is the difference between narration and asking questions about what the child did during a day or about what he saw/did when he went places? Would Charlotte Mason ask younger children any questions at all?**

You're right, we should not require a child younger than six to narrate. Charlotte said, "Until he is six, let Bobbie narrate only when and what he has a mind to. He must not be called upon to *tell* anything" (Vol. 1, p. 231). Of course, most children will freely and readily tell you about something that has interested them, and when that happens we can happily accept their informal narrations. But we need to be careful that we don't inadvertently convey a "performance" mind-set when asking them to tell.

It comes down to a matter of our motives, I think. We need to examine why we are asking him to tell. If we simply want to share in the child's experience, we can enter into a free discussion of what happened and what he thought about it. But if our underlying motive is somehow performance based—if we are asking him to tell something so he can show off for relatives or company or so he can validate the good job we're doing or possibly so he can practice narrating—we are erring on the side of manipulating. We are not respecting the child as a person and we may be influencing him to possibly view narration as a trick to be performed for praise rather than a valuable tool to be used for self-education.

Now, all of that seems a bit heavy, doesn't it? After all, we just asked, "Bobbie, tell Daddy what we did today." But we all know that it is the little things that can add up to become a major influence in their young hearts and minds. So let's encourage the little ones to share their thoughts when they want to, but be careful of making that retelling a matter of performance during the early years.

Narration Question #39: How do we begin narration with younger kids when they are first starting?

Two bits of advice. First, keep the passage short. This is especially important for young beginners. They can comprehend long stories by this age, but don't ask them to narrate a long passage yet.

Second, follow the steps to successful narration:

1. Make sure you choose a good living book or passage, one that the student will be able to see in his mind's eye as you read (the short passage!) aloud.

2. If the passage is a continuation of what you read last time, do a brief review.

3. Give a short introduction to the reading. Display two or three key words for the student to listen for.

4. Read the (short!) passage once and ask the student to tell you the story himself, in his own words. Close the book and listen with an encouraging look on your face as he narrates. Keep the key words on display so he can use them as a mental hook on which to hang his narration.

5. Give a simple wrap-up comment or discussion point if desired.

(See chapters 2–6 in this book for a review of those steps.)

Narration Question #40: With littles just learning to write, how do you handle it when they do not want to dictate any longer, but say, "Mom, help me to write 'X'." When that "X" is about 8 sentences long, far beyond their ability to write themselves without frustration?

It can be a helpful practice to write a child's narration as he dictates his thoughts to you. Especially during the younger grades, while the child is still getting his handwriting stabilized and fluid, it is best to stick with oral narrations.

Sometimes children, however, want to jump to writing their narrations earlier than would be best for them. I'm glad you recognize that they probably would not be able to write eight sentences with full attention and in their best handwriting without fatigue. Most littles are not at that stage. If you feel the narration should be written down, you could write the eight sentences for the student and allow him to select one of the eight to copy. Another idea might be to leave a space for one missing word in each sentence as you write it. Then write the eight missing words on index cards or scratch paper, and allow the child to find the word that belongs in each sentence and copy it in its correct place.

But also keep in mind that we do not need to write down every oral narration a child gives. Indeed, waiting on us to write or type what he says could impede a child's train of thought. If you are certain that you need some kind of record or "paper trail" for reporting purposes, you can still encourage oral narration by letting the child speak into an audio recorder or a video recorder at times and keep those files for your records.

Bonus Question: Is narration too hard for young children?

On the contrary, narration is a natural action for young children. When they are interested or excited about something, they will talk your ear off giving you all the details and their impressions of it! Charlotte simply saw the potential in that action—the potential to harness it as a tool and use it intentionally to facilitate learning.

Now, even though narration is a natural skill, it is also an art form when done well. As the children learn and grow using this method, they will fine tune their word choices, sentence structures, sequencing of thoughts, presentation, and phrasing. But all of that is a gradual process. The place to start is with their faltering, sometimes stumbling attempts.

Keep in mind the end goal: self-education with this tool. Let that goal guide your responses now. Treat those first attempts at narration as valuable educative activities. Don't heap on flattery or excessive praise, but seek to enter into the ideas and recognize the privilege of sharing in another person's learning process. Encourage, yes; flatter, no. Respect the child as a person, no matter how young.

Chapter 18
Beginning with Older Children

In chapter 17 we talked about some ideas for getting started using narration with younger children. In this chapter let's address some questions about starting the method with older children.

Narration Question #41: In the Fall I will have a 4th and 1st grader. I am going to try to have my 4th grader be more independent and therefore she will be reading more subjects/books on her on and then narrating her books to me. However there will be an overlap of the books they both will hear. I know when you are starting out with narration in 1st grade, it is recommended to start with Aesop's Fables. Do I still need to do this or can I have him narrate some of the science books that I will be reading to him instead of the Fables?

If your first grader has grown up hearing the books you've been reading aloud to his older sibling (and hearing her narrate), you might not need to start with fables. They are conducive to beginners because they contain a whole story in just a paragraph or two. But you could try using the shared book you mentioned and adjust the portions you read according to the children's experience with narration. For example, you could read a paragraph or two and ask the first grader to narrate; then continuing from there, read a longer portion and ask the fourth grader to narrate. As time allows, keep going with the readings, alternating and mixing up the order of short and long and who you ask to narrate.

Also, make sure you do the short review/introduction before you read in order to set the children—but especially your beginner—up for success. It will help greatly if you give him that framework on which to hang what he is hearing and narrating.

Narration Question #42: How should I begin narration if I am starting with older children who have not done it from the beginning?

If this will be their first exposure to the method of narration, I would recommend you take some time up front to explain what you will be requiring and why. This is a foreign concept to them, and it's only fair to let them know what to expect. Tell them that you will be reading the passage only once and you expect them to listen carefully and pay full attention. Explain how much time that habit will save and how quickly they will be done with their schoolwork if they acquire it. Tell them the secret of picturing the living book's passage in their minds' eyes as they listen, then words will come easily when it is time to retell. Explain what narration is and why you will be asking them to narrate. Present narration as a powerful learning tool that they will be able to use the rest of their lives to help them learn for themselves.

Narration Question #43: How would you begin with older students: middle and high school levels?

If the students are old enough to do the reading independently, which would most likely be the case with this age group, you may want to carve out some time during the beginning weeks to sit with them as they do their silent reading in order to help them set up good habits. In particular, you will want to encourage them to read the passage only once and to give it their full attention. You could even take their longer reading assignments and break them into shorter segments, asking for a narration after each segment.

Of course, be careful of your demeanor as you sit with them. You don't want them to feel like you are breathing down their necks or impatient for them to finish. Rather, you want your presence to convey an attitude like that of a supportive and encouraging personal trainer.

Narration Question #44: When starting with a middle-school student, what's the best way to begin? Do I start with oral narration and then move into written? Is it better to start with read-alouds or with books she is reading independently, or both?

I usually recommend doing oral narrations first until the student gets comfortable and fluent in the method, then moving to written. This process allows the students to practice the mental work of composition the Charlotte Mason way. Especially if they are used to writing formulaic, analytical, dry book-report-type assignments, you will want to have a way to help them easily make the transition to thinking in ideas. Telling you their thoughts will be much faster and less frustrating than toiling to get them all on paper only to find out later that it's not what you had in mind. In other words, oral narration will give you the benefit of listening to the students' thoughts, evaluating their comprehension, and guiding them through the process of learning how to narrate in "real time." Once they understand it and feel comfortable with it, they can move to writing their narrations for your time-delayed feedback.

As far as whether to start with read-alouds or independent silent reading, some of that decision depends on the student. If he is most comfortable with reading for himself, allow him to do that with your supportive presence ready at hand. (See answer to Narration Question #43.) If your student would feel more comfortable learning this new skill by listening to you read aloud, do so until he finds his feet and is ready to take over the reading for himself.

In the next chapter we will take a closer look at written narrations and answer your questions about that topic. I hope this Narration Q & A section is helping you think through the ins and outs of this powerful yet simple method.

Bonus Question: My child prefers listening to me read over reading for herself. Should I urge her toward independent reading or continue to read aloud to her?

As a student gains reading fluency, she should start to read more of her school books for herself. Charlotte began that transition for her students when they were about ten years old. You do want to encourage independent silent reading, if the student is capable of it, for three important reasons. First, reading for herself allows the student to see how words are spelled. It will be difficult for her to progress in spelling if she rarely sees the words. Second, independent reading allows the student to process at her own pace. Third, the more the student reads for herself and narrates what she has read, the closer she will move toward establishing the habit of self-education.

Now, having said that, keep in mind that some people can absorb information better when they hear it than when they read it. That's not to say those people should not be required to read for themselves; reading independently is crucial to self-education. However, if your child leans toward being an auditory learner, you might encourage her sometimes by giving her an audio version along with the printed copy and letting her listen as she follows along in the book.

Chapter 19
Written Narration: The Next Step in Composition

We've been discussing oral narration for several chapters now. It's time to move on to the next step in composition.

Wait a minute! you say to yourself. *The next step? I thought written narration was composition.*

So often when we discuss composition, we focus on the writing. Writing is, indeed, a part of composition, but another part comes first: the mental work.

Here's a challenge for you. Ready? Grab a sheet of paper and write a composition on the topic, "My Favorite Kitchen Appliance." Go.

Did you immediately start writing the introduction? Probably not. You most likely started thinking about it first: *What is my favorite kitchen appliance? Why is it my favorite? Why is she asking me to write about this anyway?*

Now think about this: Charlotte called oral narration "oral composition." All the time that our students are doing oral narration, they are practicing the necessary mental process of composition. When they and their handwriting fluency are ready, they can transition neatly to the next step: writing down their thoughts.

With that in mind, let's answer some questions.

From Oral Composition to Written Composition

Narration Question #45: When and how should I make the transition to having my child do written narrations?

Look for basically three signs that the student is ready for written narration: (1) fluent in oral narrations, which shows that the mental process is in place; (2) comfortable in handwriting techniques, so he doesn't have to concentrate on letter formation as well as content; (3) a good mental storehouse of word spellings from copywork and transcription, so he will be able to spell many of the words he wants to use. Charlotte made the transition when the student was around ten years old.

An easy way to make the transition is to tell the student that from here out you will be asking him to write one of his narrations each week. (That's not a magic number; it's just a suggestion.) If he falters and hesitates and shows signs of blank-white-sheet-of-page writer's block, try this little technique: Have him start narrating orally as usual, and you write or type what he is dictating. When he gets near the end—maybe one or two sentences left—stop writing and hand him the paper. Tell him to finish it. The task won't look so daunting now that most of it is already done and he knows what he's going to say. Over time, you can stop sooner and sooner until he is writing the whole thing himself.

Narration Question #46: How does one properly correct a narration for errors—both written and oral?

It's important to keep in mind that narration is an art as well as a natural skill. Allow time for that art to develop over the years. Therefore, approach corrections gently and incrementally. Don't penalize the student for something you haven't taught him yet. Encourage him by pointing out what he did well, not just his errors. Some practical specifics are below.

Narration Question #47: Should I be correcting my child's written narrations?

Yes, once he has settled into the process of getting his thoughts down on paper. You don't want to discourage his efforts by grabbing a red pen and "bleeding" all over his composition, but you do want to help him improve over time. I recommend focusing on just one or two points at a time. For example, you could start with beginning a sentence with a capital letter. Talk about that guideline, then hold him responsible for it in future narrations. If he overlooks it, point it out and have him make the needed changes in his writing. Continue until he has mastered that guideline, then move on to another point.

Narration Question #48: How do we know what needs to be corrected for our children if we are not that great at writing?

Grab a reference book that has concise, straightforward guidelines that you can use as a framework. *Write Right* by Jan Venolia has a helpful section on capitalization and punctuation, as well as some tips on the craft of writing. For high schoolers, I heartily recommend *The Elements of Style* by William Strunk, Jr., and E. B. White (yes, the author of *Charlotte's Web*).

Narration Question #49: Is there some kind of guide you recommend for the teacher to use to help our children improve upon their written narrations?

Look through your reference book and make a list of the guidelines that you think are common (used most often) and are important to communicating clearly. Those will be your base line. Choose one or two to start with and begin the process of incrementally introducing them and holding the student responsible to follow them in his narrations. As he demonstrates mastery, introduce another while still holding him responsible for all the previous ones.

Some teachers find it helpful to make a rubric that outlines the components that the student should be including in his writing. With that tool both the teacher and the student knows what is expected and can evaluate whether he is improving.

You can find many rubric examples online. Be sure to customize it with your selected guidelines as you go along. Some sample rubrics may be found on pages 70–73.

Narration Question #50: Do you recommend any specific resources to assist the student's writing of a narration?

Four resources come to mind:

1. Reading well-written living books. Nothing will shape your student's writing more than what he reads.

2. Pointing out one or two guidelines that will help him improve his writing. This can easily be done with dictation passages. When reading through the new exercise, take a moment to point out a guideline. Even better, help the student discover the guideline and create his own master list of punctuation and capitalization uses to remember.

3. Giving consistent practice and encouraging feedback. It's all too easy to allocate written narrations to the hit-and-miss category of assignments. For steady improvement, the student needs steady writing opportunities with ongoing attention. It doesn't have to be elaborate, but it does need to be consistent.

4. Continuing some oral narrations. As the number of written narrations increases, don't abandon oral narrations. Oral narration will give the student continuing practice in that mental process and a nice change of pace to keep variety in his schoolwork.

In the next chapter we will take a look at how to increase the challenge of narrating as the students progress.

Bonus Question: My child likes to tell me his narration and then go write it down. Is that okay?

For some children, it might be easier to write their narration after doing an oral narration first. I don't think it's a problem as long as it is a transition step. Eventually you want your child to be able to work independently, without the step of waiting for you to be available to tell, especially when he is reading his school book assignments silently for himself. You may want to gradually wean your student away from telling you his "rough draft" and encourage him to tell it in his head or even out loud to himself quietly in another room where he won't disturb anyone else.

A Possible Rubric for Beginning Writers

Content: to communicate knowledge		Possible Points	Awarded Points
Thorough	Key points are included	10	
Accurate	Facts are correct. Demonstrates that the student has read and understands the material.	10	
Original	Student uses primarily his own words.	10	
Mechanics: to communicate clearly			
Capitalization	At the beginning of each sentence.	10	
Punctuation	Appropriate mark at the end of each sentence.	10	
Spelling	Subtract 1 point for each misspelled word. Stop at 0 points awarded.	10	
Grammar & Form	Sentence breaks make it easy to follow the line of thought.	10	
Style: to communicate effectively			
Assignment	Written in narrative or expository style as assigned.	10	
Logical	Narrative relates the story events in the correct sequence. Expository gives the explanation in workable/logical steps.	10	
Cohesive	Focused on the topic. Does not wander. Does not insert unneeded filler.	10	
TOTAL		100	

A Possible Rubric for Progressing Writers

Content: to communicate knowledge		Possible Points	Awarded Points
Thorough	Key points are included.	10	
Accurate	Facts are correct. Demonstrates that the student has read and understands the material.	10	
Original	Student uses primarily his own words. Personal connections or ideas are included.	10	
Mechanics: to communicate clearly			
Capitalization	At the beginning of each sentence and for proper names.	10	
Punctuation	Appropriate mark at the end of each sentence. Correct dialogue punctuation. Correct use of apostrophes in possessives and contractions.	10	
Spelling	Subtract 1 point for each misspelled word. Stop at 0 points awarded.	10	
Grammar & Form	Sentence breaks make it easy to follow the line of thought. Verb tense consistent throughout. Number agreement between subject & verb and pronoun & antecedent.	10	
Style: to communicate effectively			
Assignment	Written in narrative, expository, or descriptive style as assigned.	10	
Logical	Narrative relates the story events in the correct sequence. Expository gives the explanation in workable/logical steps. Descriptive moves from overview to details.	10	
Cohesive	Focused on the topic. Does not wander. Does not insert unneeded filler. Well-structured introduction and conclusion.	10	
TOTAL		100	

A Possible Rubric for Experienced Writers

Content: to communicate knowledge		Possible Points	Awarded Points
Thorough	Key points are included.	10	
Accurate	Facts are correct. Demonstrates that the student has read and understands the material.	10	
Original	Student uses primarily his own words. Personal connections, ideas, and opinions are included.	10	
Mechanics: to communicate clearly			
Capitalization	At the beginning of each sentence and for proper names. Correct capitalization in dialogues.	10	
Punctuation	Appropriate mark at the end of each sentence. Correct dialogue punctuation. Correct use of apostrophes in possessives and contractions. Clarifying commas and semicolons used (to separate independent clauses, set off extra information, signify series).	10	
Spelling	Subtract 1 point for each misspelled word. Stop at 0 points awarded.	10	
Grammar & Form	Sentence breaks make it easy to follow the line of thought. Verb tense consistent throughout. Number agreement between subject & verb and pronoun & antecedent. Modifiers placed in best location for clarity. Pronoun use correct and clear. Paragraph breaks make it easy to follow the line of thought.	10	

Style: to communicate effectively			
Assignment	Written in narrative, expository, descriptive, or persuasive style as assigned.	10	
Logical	Narrative relates the story events in the correct sequence. Expository gives the explanation in workable/logical steps. Descriptive moves from overview to details. Persuasive states the thesis and gives supporting points.	10	
Cohesive	Focused on the topic. Does not wander. Does not insert unneeded filler. Well-structured introduction and conclusion. Smooth transitions between paragraphs.	10	
TOTAL		100	

Chapter 20
Raising the Bar

Can you touch your ceiling? I can't touch the ceiling in my kitchen even if I jump. It's a standard height, but I can barely reach it with a 2-foot-long fly swatter.

Now can you imagine jumping over your ceiling? That's the current world record for high jump: a smidgen over 8 feet.

I daresay the man who holds that record didn't start clearing the bar at 8 feet on his first try. In high jump—as well as most other sports—achieving the goal is a gradual process. You start with the bar lower as you learn and practice the technique. Then as you master that level, the bar is raised a little higher and you work toward clearing it. Once that height is mastered, it is raised a little higher still, then even higher, until pretty soon those lower heights seem too easy.

So it is with narration.

How to Raise the Bar

Narration is not just "retell the story" forever and ever, even into high school. No. We are expected to raise the bar on our children's narrations as they grow older and more experienced.

Narration Question #51: What are the characteristics of a good narration? Is it important that they have a clear beginning, middle and end of the story? Does it have to be in complete sentences? What other specifics would define a good narration?

What you have mentioned are ways of incrementally raising the bar. As your children grow comfortable with the concept of telling back in their own words, you can introduce higher expectations. Keep in mind that improvement in narration will be a process that requires practice, just as any other skill does; so encourage growth, model your expectations, guide as needed, but try not to criticize or discourage the children. Ultimately, yes, we want correct recall, logical progression, complete and well-crafted sentences, originality of style potentially sprinkled with the author's phrasing at poignant times, but many of those details will come with prolonged exposure to good writing (in the living books they read) and practice narrating. Keep those goals in mind, but give the children plenty of time to achieve that height.

What characteristics or goals you have in mind can depend on what type of narration you are asking for. Read on.

Narration Question #52: Can you briefly outline what depth of narration we should expect at different ages? Specifically, how will an upper elementary narration differ from a middle school narration, and how will a middle school narration differ from a high school narration?

When I was doing the research for our complete Charlotte Mason language arts reference book, *Hearing and Reading, Telling and Writing*, I compiled a list of narration questions that Charlotte gave as examples. Once that list was complete, I discovered something that fascinated me: Charlotte raised the bar as the children got older by asking for different types of narration. Most composition courses cover the same four types of writing: narrative, expository, descriptive, and persuasive. Charlotte didn't need a separate composition course to teach those ways of communication. She incorporated them simply in the way she worded narration questions, and she introduced them gradually as the children advanced through the grade levels.

So following her example, an older student should be required to narrate in different ways, not just retell the story. Here is a brief overview of the natural progression.

- Grades 1–3: Narrative, asking the student to retell the plot in chronological order.
- Grades 4–6: (Continue some narrative and add) Expository, asking the student to give a clear and accurate explanation of how something works.
- Grades 7–9: (Continue narrative and expository and add) Descriptive, asking the student to describe something, usually progressing from large scope to smaller details.
- Grades 10–12: (Continue narrative, expository, descriptive and add) Persuasive, asking the student to state his opinion and give supporting points in a logical manner.

Narration Question #53: Can you give examples of narration prompts for middle and then high school so we see how they change with our children's developing critical thinking skills?

Narration Question #54: Examples of specific written narration prompts for older kids would be beneficial. That transition time from tell me all you know to compare and contrast, etc. seems to be a sticking point with many.

On pages 78-80 are some of the narration questions I found in Charlotte's writings. Where possible, I highlighted her specific topics or removed them and inserted generic descriptive phrases so you could repurpose the questions more easily.

Narration Question #55: How do we come up with narration questions that are more than "tell back what you read," especially if you have not read the material thoroughly yourself? Instead of having a separate writing course, I've always wanted to study a certain form of writing and then apply it to the daily narrations for that week, but I'm not sure how to work that out practically.

Of course, there is no substitute for reading the material yourself. The more familiar you are with the reading, the more detailed you can make your narration request. However, certain genres lend themselves well to certain types of narrations. For example, biographies, living history books, and Bible readings often provide good opportunities for narratives or for persuasive opinions and comparisons between characters; living geography books often lean toward descriptive narrations; and living science books toward expository or descriptive questions. So if you know the genre and the topic, you may be able to craft an appropriate narration question that is a higher level than just "tell the story"; but to really raise the bar, you'll want to read for yourself and get the details.

Bonus Question: Are there other ways we can vary narration assignments besides asking for the four types of narration?

Yes. As you look through the questions that Charlotte asked her students on the following pages, you will also see that she challenged them to try their hands at various styles of writing. For example, she sometimes asked for a narration to be written in poetry form (and if she really wanted to raise the bar, she would ask for the poetry to be written in the style of a particular poet whom the students had been reading lately). She gave them opportunity to write diary entries, letters, script scenes, and more. The possibilities are vast!

Narration Questions Charlotte Used

(compiled from Vol. 3, pp. 272–299, 312, 318 and Vol. 6, pp. 178, 193, 194, 203–208)

It is helpful to know what kinds of questions Charlotte used when asking for narrations. This list is a compilation of questions she used for end-of-term written narration/compositions.

I have tried to generalize the wording in these questions so as to make them useable in a variety of situations. Generalizations are in italics. In places where generalizations did not come easily, original wording was kept but italicized to show where you could substitute your own wording.

Notice how Charlotte incorporated the four main composition types in her narration questions.

- Narrative—Telling a story, either fact or fiction.
- Expository—Informing, or explaining a subject.
- Descriptive – A type of expository writing. Painting a picture by incorporating imagery and specific details.
- Persuasive—Stating an opinion and attempting to influence the reader.

Charlotte asked for mostly Narrative and Expository compositions in the earlier grades: "Tell the story . . ."; "What do you know . . ."; Tell how . . . ."

In the older grades Charlotte added Descriptive and Persuasive compositions: "Describe . . ."; "Discuss . . ."; "Write a letter to a newspaper . . . ."

Grades 1–3

- Tell the story of . . .
- Tell a *fairy* story.
- What have you noticed (yourself) about [*an object of nature studied*]?
- Gather three sorts of [*nature object studied*] and tell all you can about them.
- Tell about . . .
- Tell all you know about . . .
- Tell what you know about . . .
- What is a *hero*? What *heroes* have you heard of? Tell about one.
- What have you noticed about [*an object of nature studied*]? Tell all you know about it.

Grades 4–6

- [*Quote from a book read*] Who said this? Tell the story.
- Tell the history of [*a current item or phrase read about*].
- What did you see in [*picture studied*]?
- [*Quote from a book read*] Of whom was this said? Tell the story. What do you know of [*historical person read about*]?
- What *towns, rivers, and castles* would you see in traveling about [*geographical area read about*]?
- How many kinds of bees are there in a hive? What work does each do? Tell how they build the comb.

Grades 7–9

- Describe the *founding of Christ's Kingdom*. What are the *laws of His Kingdom*?
- Explain [*key phrase from historical event*] and give an account of [*related historical event read about*].
- What do you know of [*historical event read about*]?
- Show fully how [*historical person read about*] acquired [*a certain title or nickname*]. Why was it a strange title for a man in those days?
- Describe a journey in [*geographical area read about*].
- How are the following seeds dispersed? Give diagrams and observations. Describe the [*part of two natural objects*].
- Give a diagram of [*body part studied*], and explain how [*it works*].
- Describe your favorite scene in [*literature book read*].
- Write twelve lines on[*historical person read about*].
- Discuss [*modern political person's*] scheme. How is it working?
- Write an essay on [*current event*], showing what some of the difficulties have been and what has been achieved.

Grades 10–12

- For what purpose were [*historical group*] instituted?

- [*Quote from historical person read about*] Write a short sketch of the character of [*historical person*], discussing the above statement.
- What do you know of the [*historical group or political party studied*]?
- Distinguish between [*pairs of related words with subtle differences of meaning*], using each word in a sentence.
- Give shortly [*author's*] estimate of [*historical person read about*], showing what [*historical person*] did for [*cause or country*] and what was the cause of his personal *failure* in life.
- Give some account, as far as you can in the style of [*author*], of [*historical event read about*].
- Write a letter in the manner of [*historical person read about*] on any Modern Topic.
- Sketch a scene between a [*famous character in literature book read*] of today and a neighbor of his.
- Describe the condition of *(a) the clergy, (b) the army, (c) the navy, (d) the general public* in and about [*time period studied*].
- Trace the rise of [*country*] before [*famous leader of that country*].
- What theories of government were held by [*historical person read about*]? Give some account of his great ministers.
- Describe the rise of [*country read about*] and its condition at [*specific time period*].
- Suppose [*historical or modern-day person in a related event*], write his diary for three days.
- Sketch the character and manners of [*character in literature book*]. How does he appear in [*historical novel*]?
- Write a letter to [*a newspaper*] on [*a current event or topic studied*].
- Write a dialogue between [*characters in a literature or history book read*].
- Write a ballad on [*current event studied*].
- Write a [*style of poetry*] on the [*current event studied*].
- Write an essay, dated [*year in the future*], on the imagined work of [*a current group or movement studied*].
- Write a woeful ballad touching the condition of [*a country studied*], or, a poem on [*a current event read about*].
- Write an essay on the present condition of [*own country*], or, on [*leader of another country*].

Chapter 21
On the Side

As we have worked our way through the Narration Q & A, I've been trying to group questions by topic. We have a couple more big topics left to cover, but first I wanted to touch on two great questions that didn't quite fit into those larger topics.

Narration Question #56: Is it acceptable for the child to have the book close by as they are writing? My 11-year-old son is always wanting the book beside him, saying that he wants to make sure he spells the names of characters correctly, or to check other spellings. He is a pretty honest child and I have seen no evidence of him copying passages from the book; I just fear the skill/act of narration is not at the same level if he is in any way re-reading passages alongside writing the narration. I have tried writing key character names, places, and such on a whiteboard for him, but he still prefers the book to be at his side.

This situation does present a bit of a conundrum, doesn't it? On the one hand, we don't want to put before him any temptation to reread the passage. On the other hand, we want to encourage correct spelling.

What you might do is continue writing key character names and places on the whiteboard for him to refer to and give him a dictionary to look up any other words' spellings as needed. You might even allow him to create a master list of words that he has looked up throughout the readings in that book and to keep that list handy for reference too. Between the list, the dictionary, and the whiteboard, there would be little need to look back in the book.

You might also keep the balance leaning toward oral narrations. Since he is 11 years old, most of his narrations can still be done orally, with only one or two written per week. An added benefit to oral narrations is that they would eliminate any need for looking in the book for correct spellings, and you would get an idea of what he knows after a single attentive reading.

You can also make sure the pre-reading reviews and end-of-term exams are being done without the book. The pre-reading review is usually oral, and with the end-of-term exams being a review of material he has already covered, he would already have had the opportunity to learn most of those spellings previously.

Narration Question #57: With narration, is there a place for note-taking?

Yes, I think there is a place for note-taking. We want to be very careful that it does not become a crutch to shore up a lack of full attention. Whenever possible, narration after a single attentive reading (or hearing) should be the rule. But some sources of material do not lend themselves well to narration, and our students may encounter those alternate sources more and more as they progress through the upper grades.

Some lectures or textbooks may present information in a way that requires note-taking. For example, if a lecturer compiles a chart on the blackboard, the student will most likely need to copy it in his notes. A chapter in chemistry that presents math equations will probably require some close work with those equations and practice for fluency, not just a one-time narration of the concept. Detailed definitions and other information-packed material may need to be copied and memorized as part of the learning process. So don't rule out note-taking as a valuable skill, but be careful that it is used only as needed and in addition to narration, not as a substitute.

(By the way, it's interesting that in Charlotte's teacher training college, the students would listen to a lecture without taking notes. At the end of class they would have a few minutes of silence to write down everything they could remember from the lecture. Quite a different expectation for note-taking than we have today!)

Bonus Question: What are the top four things to remember when doing a narration lesson?

"A few pedagogic maxims should help us, such as, 'Do not explain,' 'Do not question,' 'Let one reading of a passage suffice,' 'Require the pupil to relate the passage he has read' " (Vol. 6, p. 304).

Chapter 22
Narration in High School

This year we graduated our third child from our home school. All three of our children were taught with Charlotte Mason methods, though I refined my techniques over the years as I researched and learned more. Some of the refinements I made were in how I used narration during the high school years. Here is what I have learned.

Narration Question #58: Is narration enough for high school level studies?

Yes. Absolutely, yes, *if* you continue to raise the bar on the types of narrations you ask for as the student progresses. Narration is a powerful and versatile tool that can be used in many ways. High-school-level work should require high-school-level narrations.

Narration Question #59: How much written narration for high school students? How many times per week, per subject? How long? How detailed? If they do a written narration, say, once or twice a week in history, chemistry, government—and they have narrated orally in between—should I be looking for a summary of the whole week's reading to put it in written form at that point? Or should it be "just" a detailed account of today's reading like the oral ones? I struggle with this one because I feel like the kids may need the act of writing and recalling periodically in order to cement the knowledge they've gained through the week.

We've dealt with some of these questions in previous chapters. Take a look at chapter 15, "Magic Numbers," and chapter 11, "The Long and Short of It," for answers on how many and how long. The level of detail you expect will depend on what type of narration you're asking for and how detailed your narration question is. (See chapter 20, "Raising the Bar.") Some of it will also depend on where the student is in his individual progression with his writing. (See chapter 19, "Written Narration: The Next Step in Composition.")

Pre-reading reviews will be crucial to the process of cementing the student's knowledge from one reading to the next. If the student is experienced in Charlotte Mason methods, he can and should be doing those pre-reading reviews on his own by high school.

Many of the persuasive-type narration questions are more wide-sweeping in their scope. Those types of questions will cover larger portions of the book and demonstrate how well the student is putting together the pieces to make the knowledge his own as he reads. I would recommend using those rather than asking for just a shortened or summary retelling.

Narration Question #60: I am comfortable with narration for Bible, literature, and history, but what do you recommend for an Apologia high school science course? I want to stick with narration (as we've done with Apologia General

Science) because comprehension of the material has been better than it was in my pre-C.M. days. Still, I am struggling with mistrusting narration for a high school level science course.

Narration is a powerful tool, but it is not the only tool. Not all resources lend themselves well to narration. As much as possible, we want to use living books that are easily narrated, but that's not always possible as our students get into the upper grades. Some material is not available in story or narrative form and some cannot be covered adequately that way—high school level science courses being one example. That material will be more effectively learned through a combination of narration and note-taking, memorizing and practicing. By all means, do not skip the narrating; use it as much as possible. But supplement it with other helpful techniques as needed. (See Narration Question #57.)

Narration Question #61: I'm most interested in narration at the high school level. Would LOVE to see samples of students at various levels, both from narration "veterans" as well as beginners.

I just read this narration sample tucked into *In Memorium: Charlotte M. Mason*, page 172, written by a girl of 15. The class read Ruskin's *Modern Painters* for twenty minutes and wrote for the remaining twenty minutes of the lesson. Here are her thoughts on "The Open Sky."

> Who can describe the sky? Those changing moods that vary from glaring noon-day heat to the soft grey dusk of evening. Never the same for two minutes together, but always changing—changing—changing. But it is not always so restless. There may be days when the torn shreds of clouds race forward before the wind, but then there comes an evening when quiet peace reigns. The sun sinks, leaving the west in a blaze of rosy colour which gradually dies away to soft drowsy blue and grey. The stars come out one by one, as though afraid to spoil that glorious peaceful blue with their insistent twinkle, and the soft dew falls to cover the sleeping earth.
>
> And yet, all this beauty leaves many people unmoved. They know the sky chiefly from pictures. If you asked them to describe it, some scrap of blue, framed with gold and hanging in some dusty corner, springs to their mind. They do not think of looking upwards into the vastness over their heads; for they do not see it in pictures. Few artists can portray the feeling of never-ending eternity that the sky has. They paint a hard beautiful blue with solid bunchy clouds. You look at it, and, instead of sailing ever on and upwards, your gaze is brought up with a jerk against a blue board.

You will find lots of sample narrations from Charlotte's own students (of all ages) in her original writings in the back of Volume 3 (*School Education*) and on pages 195 and following of Volume 6 (*Philosophy of Education*). We have included a few on pages 87–96 of this book, along with some samples from modern-day students.

Narration Question #62: How do high school students learn to write the various forms of papers?

The main forms that come to mind are the research paper and the five-paragraph essay. You may think of others, but either way I would share these three tips.

First, rather than jumping directly into How, I would recommend you start with Why: Why does my student need to learn to write those two forms of papers? Not all students will need to—mainly only those planning on taking college level courses.

Second, if you have determined that your student does, indeed, need to learn how to format a research paper and a five-paragraph essay, keep in mind that it doesn't take twelve years to learn those formats. They can easily be learned in a short amount of time. If the student knows how to write in an expository, descriptive, and persuasive way, he has already achieved the biggest part of the goal. All that would be left is to fashion his composition into the expected format.

Third, look for a concise resource that will walk your student through the process of learning those formats. Longer is not necessarily better; straight-forward and to-the-point is best. Remember, he already knows how to write; he is just learning the format that will be expected. Ideally, the resource will use good literature in its lessons or will allow you to assign your own topics for writing and you can give assignments based on the student's regular good-living-book readings.

In the past we have recommended two short courses from Analytical Grammar: *Teaching the Essay* and *Teaching the Research Paper*. Those short courses have recently been revised and are now both included in their new *Beyond the Book Report, Season Three* resource, along with the personal essay, the SAT essay, and preparing an oral presentation with digital slides.

Bonus Question: How important is it that my student excel in composition?

It seems like this subject is one that can easily become a stumbling block. Many parents and teachers give the impression that composition is the end-all-be-all of a student's education. *If he can't write well, he's not well educated* seems to be the default attitude. While we need to encourage our students to do their best to communicate accurately and clearly, we also need to give honor to the person God has made each student to be. Not everyone will have the same ability in composition. Not everyone will best communicate through the medium of the written word. That's okay. Monet is not well known for his essays, nor Beethoven for his research papers. God has given different people different talents and abilities, and part of our job as parents is to help our children identify and hone those talents so they can be used for the benefit of others and the glory of God. Keeping a balanced perspective is best.

Sample Narrations

Oral narration by a 7-year-old to the question: What have you noticed (yourself) about a spider? (as recorded in Vol. 3, p. 274)

We have found out the name of one spider, and often have seen spiders under the microscope—they were all very hairy. We have often noticed a lot of spiders running about the ground—quantities. Last term we saw a spider's web up in the corner of the window with a spider sucking out the juice of a fly; and we have often touched a web to try and make the spider come out, and we never could, because she saw it wasn't a fly, before she came out.

I saw the claw of a spider under the microscope, with its little teeth; we saw her spinnerets and her great eyes. There were the two big eyes in one row, four little ones in the next row, and two little ones in the next row. We have often found eggs of the spiders; we have some now that we have got in a little box, and we want to hatch them out, so we have put them on the mantelpiece to force them.

Once we saw a spider on a leaf, and we tried to catch it, but we couldn't; he immediately let himself down on to the ground with a thread.

We saw the circulation in the leg of another spider under the microscope; it looked like a little line going up and down.

Oral narration by an 8-year-old to the question: What have you noticed about a thrush? Tell all you know about it. (as recorded in Vol. 3, pp. 279, 280)

Thrushes are browny birds. They eat snails, and they take the snail in their mouths and knock it against a stone to break the shell and eat the snail. I found a stone with a lot of bits of shell round it, so knew that a thrush had been there. Where we used to live a thrush used to sing every morning on the same tree. The song of the thrush is like a nightingale. We often see a lot of thrushes on the lawn before breakfast or after a shower. They have yellow beaks and their breasts are specked with lovely yellow and brown. Once we found a thrush asleep on a sponge in a bedroom and we carried it out and put it on a tree. Thrushes eat worms as well as snails, and on the lawn they listen with their heads on one side and go along as the worm gets under the ground, and presently, perhaps, the worm comes up and they gobble it up, or they put their beaks in and get it. Thrushes build their nests with sticks at the bottom and line them with little bits of wool they pick up, or feathers, and they like to get down very much.

Oral narration by a 9-year-old to the question: What did you see in the *Seagull* sailing up the Firth of Forth? (Book studied, *Geographical Reader,* Book II.) (as recorded in Vol. 3, p. 282)

In sailing up the Forth we first of all see Leith, which is the seaport town of Edinburgh. Then we come to Edinburgh. The old and new Edinburghs are built on opposite hills, the valley in between is laid out in lovely gardens. One thing very odd about Edinburgh is that the streets look as if they are built one on top of the other. At one end of the town there is a castle which looks so like the rocks and mountains it is built on, one can hardly distinguish it. At the other end of the town there is Holyrood, where the ancient kings used to live. We do not see many merchantmen because there are no good harbours, there are a good many fishing smacks and pleasure boats. As we go along we see women with big baskets with a strap across their foreheads, and they are calling out "caller herrings."

Oral narration by a 10-year-old to the question: How many kinds of bees are there in a hive? What work does each do? Tell how they build the comb. (Book studied, *Fairyland of Science*.) (as recorded in Vol. 3, p. 285)

Three kinds. The *drones* or males, the *workers* or females, and the *queen* bee. The drone is fat, the queen is long and thin, the workers are small and slim. The queen bee lays the eggs, the worker bee brings the honey in and makes the cell, and the drones wait to be fed. On a summer's day you see something hanging on a tree like a plum pudding, this is a swarm of bees. You will soon see someone come up with a hive, turn it upside down, shake the bough gently, and they will fall in. They will put some clean calico quickly over the bottom of the hive, and turn it back over on a bench. The bees first close up every little hole in the hive with wax, then they hang on to the roof, clinging on to one another by their legs. Then one comes away and scrapes some wax from under its body, and bites it in its mouth until it is pulled out like ribbon, this she plasters on the roof of the hive, then she flies out to get honey, and comes home to digest it, hanging from the roof, and in 24 hours this digested honey turns to wax, then she goes through the same process again. Next, the nursing bees come and poke their heads into this wax, bite the wax away (20 bees do this before one hole is ready to make a cell). Other bees are working on the other side at the same time. Each cell is made six-sided, so as to take up the least wax and the smallest space. When the cells are made the bees come in with honey in their honey-bag or first stomach; they can easily pass the honey back though their mouths into the cells. It takes many bees to fill one cell, so they are hard at work.

Written narration by a 12-year-old to the question: Describe your favourite scene in *Waverley*. (as recorded in Vol. 3, pp. 292–294) The symbol *(sic)* notates misspelled words that were intentionally left as originally written for you to see.

A Highland Stag Hunt.—The Highland Cheifs (*sic*) were in various postures: some reclining lazily on their plaids, others stalking up and down conversing with one another, and a few were already seated in position for the sport. MacIvor was talking with another Cheif (*sic*) as to what the sport would be; but as they talked in Gaelic,

Edward had no part in the conversation, but sat looking at the scene before him. They were seated on a low hill at the head of a broad valley which narrowed into a small opening or cleft in the hills at the extreme end. It was hemmed in on all sides by hills of various heights. It was through this opening that the beaters were to drive the deer. Already Waverly (*sic*) could hear the distant shouts of the men calling to each other coming nearer and nearer. Soon he could distinguish the antlers of the deer moving towards the opening like a forest of trees stiped (*sic*) of their leaves. The sportsmen prepared themselves to give them a warm reception, and all were ready as the deer entered the valley.

They looked very ferocious, as they advanced towards where Edward and the cheifs (*sic*) were standing and seemed as if they were determined to fight; the roes and weaker ones in the centre, and the bulls standing as if on defence. As soon as they came within range, some of the cheifs (*sic*) fired, and two or three deer came down. Waverly (*sic*) also had the good fortune (and also the skill) to bring down a couple and gain the aplause (*sic*) of the other sportsmen. But the herd was now charging furiously up the valley towards them. The order was given to lie down, as it was impossible to stem the coming wave of deer; but as it was given in Gaelic it conveyed no meaning to Edward's mind, and he remained standing.

The heard (*sic*) was now not fifty yards from him; and in another minute he would have been trampled to death; but MacIvor at his own risk, jumped up and literaly (*sic*) dragged him to the ground just as the deer reached them. Edward had a sensation as if he was out in a severe hail storm, but this did not last long.

When they had passed, and Edward attempted to rise, he found that besides a number of bruises he had also severely sprained his ancle (*sic*), and was unable to walk, or even stand. A shelter was soon made for him out of a plaid in which he was laid; and then MacIvor called the Highland doctor or herbalist, to attend him. The doctor approached Edward with every sign of humiliation, but before attending to his ancle (*sic*), he insisted upon walking slowly round him several times, in the direction in which the sun goes, muttering at the same time a spell over him as he went, and though Waverly (*sic*) was in great pain he had to submit to his foolery. Waverly (*sic*) saw to his great astonishment that MacIvor believed or seemed to believe in the old man's cantations (*sic*). At last, when he had finished his spells, which he seemed to think more necessary than the dressing, he drew from his pocket a little packet of herbs, some of which he applied to the sprained ancle (*sic*) and after it had been bound up, Edward felt much relieved. He rewarded the doctor with some money, the value of which seemed to exceed his wildest imaginations, for he heaped so many blessings upon the head of Waverly (*sic*) that MacIvor said, "A hundred thousand curses on you," whereupon he stopped.

Written narration by a 13-year-old to the question: Show fully how Aristides acquired the title of "The Just." Why was it a strange title for a man in those days? (Book studied, Plutarch's *Lives: Aristides.*) (as recorded in Vol. 3, pp. 289, 290) The symbol *(sic)* notates misspelled words that were intentionally left as originally written for you to see.

Aristides acquired the title of "The Just" by his justice, and because he never did anything unjust in order to become rich or powerful. While many of the judges and chief men in Athens took bribes, he alone always refused to do so, and he also never spent the public money on himself. When, after having defeated the Persians, at Platae, the Greek States decided to have a standing army, it was Aristides who was sent round to settle how much each town should contribute. And he did this so fairly and well, that all the Greek States blessed and praised his arrangement. It is said that Aristides could not only resiste (*sic*) the unjust claims of those whom he loved, but also those of his enemies. Once when he was judging a quarrel between two men, one of them remarked that the other had often injured Aristides. "Tell me not that," was the reply of Aristides, "but what he has done to thee, for it is thy cause I am judging, not my own." Another time when he had gone to law himself, and when, after having heard what he had to say, his judges were going to pass sentence on his adversary without having heard him, Aristides rose and entreated his judges to hear what his enemy could say in his own defence. In all that he did Aristides was inflexibly Just, and many stories were told of his justice. Though he loved his country well, he would never do anything wrong to gain for Athens some advantage, and in all he did his one aim was justice, and his only ambition to be called "The Just." He was so just and good, that he was called the "most just man in Greece." In the times in which Aristides lived, men used to care more to be called great, rich, or powerful than just. Themistocles, the great rival of Aristides, used to do all he could to become the first man in Athens, and rich as well as powerful. He did not hesitate to take bribes, and all he did for the Athenians was done with a view to making himself the head of the people, and the first man in the State. He used often to do unjust as well as cruel things in order to get his own ends. It was the same with most other men who lived at this time, they prefered (*sic*) being rich, powerful or great, to being distinguished by the title of "The Just."

Written narration by a 15-year-old to the question: "His power was to assert itself in deeds, not words." Write a short sketch of the character of Cromwell, discussing the above statement. (Book studied, *Green's Shorter History of the English People.*) (as recorded in Vol. 3, p. 295) The symbol *(sic)* notates misspelled words that were intentionally left as originally written for you to see.

Cromwell was no orator. It has been said that if all his speeches were taken and made into a book, it would seem simply a pack of nonsense. In Parliament though, the earnestness with which he spoke attracted attention. His deeds proved his innate power, which could not express itself in words. He may be called the inarticulate man. In his mind, everything was clear, and his various actions proved his purposes and determinations, but in speaking, he simply brought out a hurried volume of words, in the mazes of which one entirely lost the point meant to be implied. Cromwell also was more of an administrator than a statesman, unspeculative and conservative. He was subject to fits of hypocondria (*sic*), which naturally had some effect on his character. He considered himself a servant of God, and acted accordingly. Undoubtedly he was under the conviction that he was carrying out the Lord's will in all he did. He was not in calm moods a bloody man, but when his anger was kindled he would spare no one. At times he would be filled with remorse for the part he had taken in the martyrdom of the king; then, again he would say it was the just punishment of heaven on Charles. In giving orders his words were curt and to the point, but in making speeches he adopted the phraseology of the Bible, which added to their ambiguity. One would think he was ambitious, for at one time he asked Whitelock: "What if a man should take upon himself to be king?" evidently having in view the regal power, and yet according to his own assertion he would rather have returned to his occupation as a farmer, than have undertaken the government of Britain. But in this, as in other acts, he recognised the call of God, (as he thought) and obeyed it.

Oral narration by a 15-year-old (with global language and developmental delays) covering a Bible story.

Zacchaeus climbed the tree to see all the bunch of people. And Zacchaeus saw Jesus. And they went into a house.

Written narration by a 16-year-old to the question: Tell about how the Unknown parts of the world began to become Known, using at least four explorers in your narrative. (Book studied, *Around the World in a Hundred Years* by Jean Fritz.)

The book I read covered at least ten explorers, but I decided to pick four key men to talk about in my narration.

Before the explorers, the known world seemed to be mostly Europe, Asia, and maybe some of Africa. Europe's trade route to India and China had been seized by the Turks, which was good incentive to find another route. The first man to sail all the way down Africa and round the horn was Bartholomew Diaz of Portugal. After he rounded the Cape of Good Hope (though he called it something like the Cape of Storms), he wanted to keep going. His crew, however, had a differing opinion. Even the stars in the southern equator were different, which wasn't a good morale booster. Diaz was forced to return. Later, a man named Vasco da Gama also rounded the horn and continued up to India. I think it was Vasco who began the tradition of giving Africa's dangerous coast a wider berth. A longer voyage, perhaps, but best for sailing.

He wasn't the most pleasant with the people he met along the way as he tried to find a guide, and there was a mess when he got to India because the king wanted gifts. The sailors had only brought some things to trade. The king may have kidnapped some of the sailors or something, but when Vasco left, he decided the way to treat these people was with war. He returned and sunk one of India's ships, passengers and all. Later he was assigned to be consul of India once Europe had a foothold, but he only held the position for maybe six months.

Christopher Columbus, also a Portugal, spent some time before he could finally get funding for his idea: sailing across the unknown Atlantic, which he thought would be another passageway to India and China. He tried Spain, but Spain was in a war.

Once the war was over, however, Queen Isabella and the King of Spain were willing to supply his voyage. They gave him three ships, and I think he also wanted to be called Commodore of the Seas or something.

Columbus did not discover America, or India or China for that matter, but he did make it across the unknown Atlantic at last. He discovered islands, and in particular some of the Central American ones, like Jamaica and Cuba. They searched for gold.

Columbus started a colony on the island he called Hispaniola, which didn't go so well. There was trouble, and when he returned later he found the colony killed by natives, who had had trouble with the colony. The colony was restarted.

There was also trouble for Columbus when a new governor was brought in, and he sent Columbus home in chains. He was released, however.

Columbus made maybe three voyages into the Atlantic, and then died in Europe at the end of his travels.

Other explorers crossed the Atlantic, discovering Brazil and North America. Ponce de Leon claimed Florida in his search for the fountain of eternal youth. Another man came from the colony settlement on Hispaniola and became a governor—in Brazil or somewheres. That man, by the help of a native guide, crossed over land to see the Pacific ocean. The native probably didn't understand why the man was so wrought up about seeing an ocean. There was also a guy named Amerigo Vespucci who explored and researched in the Brazil area. The Americas are actually named after him, due to a mapmaker.

Magellan is the last explorer in the book, and the last one I want to highlight. He wanted to sail to the Spice Islands, and he wanted to do it in a different way—finding a passage through the Americas. He obtained ships for this purpose, and he seemed to give the impressions that he knew where this passage would be, and maintained that view. He was also a secretive captain who liked to keep things to himself, which caused trouble with the crews. After crossing the Atlantic, they traveled down the coast of Brazil but were caught by winter. Magellan decided they would anchor in a bay for the winter—or at least that was what the crew gathered from his actions. There was a mutiny in the bay, but Magellan emerged victorious and some mutineers were left on the shore.

During their stay, they encountered giant men they called Patagonians, which means they had big feet. Actually, the Patagonians wrapped things around their feet, which is what gave that appearance.

When spring came, the ships set out again. When they encountered a kind of bay or fjord or something, Magellan sent in a ship to investigate. It turned out to be the strait! The ships entered the strait, which proved to be a twisting maze of water. Finally, though, they found the way through. Magellan actually teared up at this.

From there, they treaded through the Pacific, missing Australia and arriving in the Japan/Philippines area. Magellan began converting the natives there to Christianity. He then decided to go to an island that had been feuding with the natives and conquer it, as it were. The natives offered help, but Magellan told them to stand and watch the Spaniards. Things did not go as Magellan planned, however. There were reefs in the water by the feuding island, which meant the soldiers had to get out of their boats and wade the rest of the way in. A horde of the feuding natives met them, and Magellan was killed.

The way the Spaniards had been communicating with the natives was through

Magellan's slave, Enrique, who was now freed because of Magellan's death. The survivors of the battle told Enrique to be their interpreter to the friendly natives. One of the sailors told him that once a slave was always a slave. Enrique responded by going to the friendly natives and then staying there.

The chief invited some of the crew to a farewell feast, where he killed them.

The ships left to round Africa and make it back home. Only a straggling remainder made it back to Europe, including a man who had documented the voyage. They had circumvented the globe.

No simple passageway was discovered, however, to pass the Americas. The straits were too complex. Later, the Panama canal was dug.

Australia was also discovered eventually. People still thought that there should be another southern continent, however, to balance the earth's equilibrium. Finally, James Cook was assigned the mission of finding out about this continent. He sailed around in the Arctic Circle but didn't find Antarctica itself. He was killed later by natives in Hawaii.

Eventually, of course, Antarctica was discovered.

Written narration by a 17-year-old to the question: How have you seen the truth of this line from Wordsworth, "the child is father to the man," in the various famous men about whom you have read? Mention at least four men, citing examples from their lives. (Book studied, *Famous Men of the 16th and 17th Century* by Robert G. Shearer.)

William Bradford is a good example of Wordsworth's line. When he was just eleven years old, he chose to forego his uncle's church and instead walk miles to a Puritan church. By going to this church, he became friends with William Brewster, another church member who became later involved in the Pilgrims' exodus along with Bradford. At a young age, Bradford began demonstrating his desire to be a Puritan, though that religion was not well-looked upon by the English government.

Blaise Pascal, also, had to begin with his studies before he could become a famous scientist. His father provided schooling for him but planned to give him geometry etc. later. Blaise had other ideas, and began discovering rules of geometry on his own. At fifteen, he published a paper on conic sections, a difficult piece of geometry.

John Winthrop's childhood prepared him to become another leader of the New World colonies. He grew up in a heavily Puritan community, and became experienced in laws and such.

Gustavus Adolphus had to have his royal military training before he could become the great leader of the Swedish army.

Another example, only in this case a woman, is Bloody Mary. She had a hard childhood, being brought up away from the castle due to Henry VII's tumult-filled family life. She became a determined Catholic, as opposed to her father's more lenient views.

Written narration by a 17-year-old to the question: Give shortly Carlyle's estimate of Burns, showing what he did for Scotland, and what was the cause of his personal failure in life. (Book studied, *Carlyle's Essay on Burns.*) (as recorded in Vol. 3, pp. 297, 298)

Carlyle looked upon Burns as one of the nicest of men and greatest of poets; rather a weak man, perhaps, but covering all his faults with his genius and kindness of heart, clever and persevering, and basely neglected and shunned by his contemporaries. It is quite extraordinary to read the world-famous poems of this poet, and to remember that he was a ploughman, and surrounded only by the most uneducated peasants and fellow-labourers, though, of course, the life of a ploughman in the hills of Scotland is far more likely to encourage poetry and reflection than the life of many a London dentist or hair-dresser far higher in rank; but it is easy to believe in fact, that Burns would have found inspirations for his genius in a flat sandy waste or a grocer's shop, and, as Carlyle says, a man or woman is not a genius unless they are extraordinary, not really inspired if such a person could have been imagined before. Robert Burns has provided Scotland for centuries at least, with plenty of national poetry, his poems are such as can be enjoyed, like flowers and trees and all things really beautiful, by old and young, stupid and clever, fishermen and prime ministers—surely that is a work of which any man would be proud!

Burns (*sic*) chief fault, if fault it can be called, and the cause of his failure in life, seems to have been a sort of bitterness against people more fortunate than himself without the art of hiding it. This, real or affected, seems very common in poets, and such an inspired man, a man with a mind greater than kings, must have felt very deeply, almost without knowing it, the "unrefinedness" of the people he loved best, and his own distance from the admirers who clustered round him later in life.

All his life, it seems, he was in a place by himself, now spending his time with his own family, acting a part all day, trying to make his relations feel him an equal, pretending to take a great interest in what he did not care for—the pigs, and cows, and porridge, seeing his own dearest friends looking at him with awe, and feeling him something above them, thinking of his "great" friends, and feeling embarrassed when he came, and more at ease without his presence.

Now, on the other hand, associating with people, high in rank and education, enjoying their friendship and praise, but feeling, be they ever so kind and familiar, that he was not their equal by birth, and that they could not treat him quite as such, however hard they might try, turning familiarity in his mind into slights, and kindness into condescension. This to a proud man must have been misery, and Burns must have been very lonely in a crowd of companions, thronged with admirers, but without a friend.

Nobody understood Burns; he shared his opinions with no one he knew. When, at the beginning of the French Revolution he expressed his delight and approval, the people who admired him were shocked, refused to speak to him, and regarded him either as mad or terribly wicked. His poems were not admired as much as they deserved to be, he had hardly any money, was never likely to get on in the world, was shunned and disgraced, and began, as a last resource, to drink too much. Ill-health was one of his misfortunes, and this intemperance killed him.

Thus died at the age of thirty-seven, poor, friendless, despised, the man who has given pleasure to thousands, and an undying collection of poems and songs to his country.

Written narration by an 18-year-old to the question: Compare and contrast Hitler and Stalin: the ways they came to power, their styles of governing, their personalities, and how their ideas affected the people of their countries. (Books studied, *Stalin* and *Hitler* by Albert Marrin.)

Hitler took over the government with his Nazi party. Stalin used false publicity to turn the people's minds towards him. As Lenin was dying, he did not want Stalin to take over. Stalin instead had himself "photoshopped" into a picture of Lenin, as if Stalin being the successor was completely natural. Both Hitler and Stalin weren't afraid to occasionally "clean out" their ranks of dreaded secret police. Even their trusted officials could grow to know too much over time, and must be replaced with fresh minds.

Once in power, Hitler concentrated on turning Germany into a vast war machine. In order to rule both countries, Stalin and Hitler knew they had to capture the minds of their people, not just their actions. Hitler encouraged German mothers to have many children, who were then sent to be trained in Nazi ways. Books were burned. Hitler was held up as a savior who would lead Germany to new glory, out of the ashes of WWI.

Stalin was essentially worshipped as a god—he had come a long way from the little boy whose mother had sent him to a monastery with the hopes him securing a church profession.

Citizens of both countries were encouraged to report anyone who seemed to be dissenting from the accepted schools of thought, or complaining about the government. Children turned against parents, sibling against sibling, etc. Stalin then had the prisoners beaten into "confessing" any cooked-up crimes he wanted them to have committed. Both Stalin and Hitler performed vast amounts of genocide, and had concentration camps or camps in eastern Siberia where prisoners were silently sent to work and die.

For a while Hitler and Stalin had an alliance, which was broken by Hitler. Germany invaded Russia, which obviously brought a halt to any uneasy friendship. Stalin ended up joining the Allies against Nazi Germany, even though he and Hitler were much alike. Perhaps too much alike.

As far as personalities go, they had some similarities and some differences. Stalin lived in obvious fear of his life, while Hitler acquired more of a reputation as indestructible after attempts on his life failed. Hitler seemed to have more of an abrasively forceful personality, while Stalin was perhaps a little more quiet, though no less deadly.

After Hitler's defeat, Germany went on to become a free country again, though it took many years after that for the Berlin wall to collapse. Russia continued under Marxist rule for many years, and maintained a tension with the US, until finally starting a process of reformation under Gorbachev. The USSR, captivated with the idea of communism being the natural progression of the world and the next hope for mankind, continued to try and spread its borders throughout the globe. Sometimes with troops, sometimes with spies who helped overturn governments.

Chapter 23
An Added Bonus

When I started homeschooling with the Charlotte Mason Method, my focus was all on the children. I thought this endeavor was about giving my children the kind of education that I hadn't received.

Little did I suspect the added bonus that awaited me.

You see, not only did my children receive a generous and enjoyable education, but I did too! How? By reading those wonderful living books ahead of them or along with them.

That's why these final questions are so important.

> **Narration Question #63: How do I keep up with or judge narrations of independent readers/older students when I haven't read everything first myself?**
>
> **Narration Question #64: When I haven't read the chapter or topic, how do I engage and comment on the narration?**
>
> **Narration Question #65: How do I comment on, ask questions, and encourage more in-depth thinking on a middle school/high school narration (where my child read the material independently), when I am not closely familiar with the reading material?**
>
> **Narration Question #66: How do I grade a narration or encourage deeper thinking on the content (middle/high school years in particular), when I truly don't know the difference between what my child included versus excluded from the reading material? (And given that one of my children has a major habit of skim reading.)**
>
> **Narration Question #67: Should I be using narration when I have not actually read the material personally? Should I use narration, but use it alongside other methods such as assigning additional non-narrated materials/readings or a workbook/test sheet?**

Part of the joy of a Charlotte Mason education is sharing in the ideas from those lovely books. A wonderful bond forms between parent and child as you grow to love knowledge together. As one of the teachers in Charlotte's schools put it:

> "No one knows so well as a teacher what a delight it is to see how the awakened mind, set aglow by the reception of a living idea, lights up the face, the quick recognition, the eager response; together the teacher and taught are sharing the same thrill of enthusiasm and enjoyment. I wish I could tell you of the countless moments of such pleasure that I have had and the bond of sympathy which this creates. Of course in order to arouse

> this eager receptivity there must be the love of knowledge and enthusiasm towards the acquiring of it for himself on the part of the teacher, for love is contagious and children do as we do" ("Miss Mason's Ideal in School Life" by Laura C. Faunce, as printed in the book *In Memorium: Charlotte M. Mason*, p. 167).

Sometimes we don't fully realize the powerful influence our personal example sets for our children. I would highly recommend that you make it a priority to read the books and enjoy them yourself. So many benefits come from that investment of time and thought! In fact, several of the benefits are written right into the questions posted above. When you read the books, you can

- keep up with your students and judge their narrations better,
- more readily engage in their narrations and comment on them intelligently,
- ask questions and encourage more in-depth thinking from them,
- grade their narrations fairly and easily,
- wield the tool of narration well and not have to resort to worksheets.

Charlotte mentioned another very important benefit of keeping up with our children's studies so we can carry on intelligent discussions with them:

"The parents themselves keep their place as heads of the family. They keep the respect of their children; for once a boy begins to look down on the intellectual status *of his parents, the entire honour and deference he owes them are at an end. Any pains taken to keep ahead should be repaid by the glow of honest pride the young people feel at every proof of intellectual power in their parents" (Vol. 5, p. 197).*

The benefits are great, yet the demands of everyday life are great too. How can we fit in time to read when we feel like we barely have time to breathe? Here are a few ideas that I hope will get you started.

- Simplify your life as much as possible and make it a priority.
- Institute a daily Rest and Read Time for everyone. Children who cannot yet read might listen to an audiobook or look at good picture books. The main rules are Stay on Your Bed and No Talking.
- Schedule one or two 15-minute reading slots into your daily routine, like Charlotte did. Maybe you can't do an extended reading time, but you could tuck two smaller sessions in between other events.
- Listen to audiobooks while walking, driving, or exercising.
- Get a book list and start working your way through it. You can see our favorite living books on the SCM Curriculum Guide at simplycharlottemason.com.

- If your children are young, their books will be shorter and more quickly read, leaving you additional time to get a head start on the books that will be coming down the road.
- If your children are older, use no-school days to get a head start. Then stay ahead by faithfully implementing the Rest and Read Time or a couple of 15-minute reading breaks each day. A little, consistently invested, will add up to a lot.
- Keep a pad of paper handy as you read books for older children so you can jot down a narration question or two after each chapter. See which of the four types of narration questions lend themselves most readily to that chapter. The more you do it, the easier it will become.
- Start a book club with some like-minded friends for the fellowship and accountability it will give.
- Just for fun, jot down the titles of the books you read during the year. I like to jot them down each month in my personal Calendar Journal. It's encouraging to look back over the year (or several years' lists) and see just how many wonderful books you have made a part of your own education and will be able to share with your children.

Index of Questions Answered

Chapter 7—The Why Behind the How

Narration Question #1: I always get the question from them, "Why do I have to tell it to you when you just read it?" I read everything to them right now.

Bonus Question: I understand that narration helps the student know, but are there any other reasons Charlotte chose to use the method?

Chapter 8—In My Own Words

Narration Question #2: What is narration exactly?

Narration Question #3: How can I get my child to stop narrating word for word/parroting passages? How can I encourage her to put it into her own words?

Bonus Question: Should I expect all of my children's narrations to be the same?

Bonus Question: Why might my child be parroting from the book?

Chapter 9—The Simplest Way

Narration Question #4: Should we require narration of the entire passage/chapter/story read? Or, should we break it down into pieces if it's longer?

Narration Question #5: If we have a child who is supposed to be reading 10 pages but can't keep up with that much information to narrate, how do we handle narration?

Narration Question #6: My question is that even though we have been doing narration for years, some of my kids will consistently automatically stop listening when I read to them and have no idea what the reading, book, story, etc. was even about. Lately I have been using audiobooks and even though they do the same thing, I replay them. I know this goes against CM habit training but we've tried the other way for years. I guess I'm asking if there's a reason I should NOT do this?

Bonus Question: How can I stop for a narration after every paragraph or two and still keep the lesson times short?

Bonus Question: Do you have a recommendation for a book to use with beginning narrators?

Chapter 10—Set Them Up for Success

Narration Question #7: What to do if the child cannot give a narration after a completed lesson, even after gentle prompts? Should the response to this situation vary with the age of the child or does it solely depend on the reason behind not being able to narrate the lesson?

Narration Question #8: We've been working on cultivating the habit of attention and best effort over the past couple months. Sometimes when I ask my child to tell back what she remembers after a brief reading she says she doesn't know what to say, but I know she listened. What do I do when she's reluctant to narrate after a first reading?

Narration Question #9: How do I encourage a younger child who consistently responds, "I don't know"?

Narration Question #10: My 13-year-old seems to freeze when I say, "Tell me about…". I really think she doesn't listen well—probably more visual like me. Any advice?

Narration Question #11: I'm trying to get started with narration with my six-year-old. She says "I don't remember" when I ask what the story was about. Do I ask leading questions to get her started?

Narration Question #12: How do I motivate my child when she just doesn't "feel" like narrating?

Bonus Question: How can I learn more about this process of setting my child up for success in a narration lesson?

Chapter 11—The Long and Short of It

Narration Question #13: How long should a narration be (on average)?

Narration Question #14: How much narration is "enough"? My 9-year-old only says about 2 sentences every time no matter the length of reading.

Narration Question #15: What about narrations that seem to take as long as the reading itself?

Narration Question #16: What to do with a child (almost 9) who can narrate about the full text literally? (About as long as I read, even with long pieces of texts). We're only just beginning to homeschool, so he needs guidance to know what is most important and to be brief. How do I direct him in that?

Narration Question #17: What do you do with children who are resistant to narrating? We are fairly new to narrating, and my 2 oldest children, ages 9 and 7, balk, complain and get irritated when I ask them to narrate back to me. I try to ask some leading questions, and they give the shortest answers possible. Or, they'll tell a one-line narration of what we just read, instead of telling the story back in their own words.

Chapter 12—Correct Me If I'm Wrong

Narration Question #18: What do I do if my child narrates back with incorrect information, especially on something like a Bible narration?

Narration Question #19: What do I do if my child is narrating things out of order?

Narration Question #20: How to encourage more indepth/detailed narration without "digging it out of them"? We've been narrating for 4 years now and I don't feel like I am getting good narrations from them. I get "She went to that place and saw him." I can get a sentence or two out of a reading. I know that they know more than that.

Narration Question #21: What do I do if my child leaves out a key point in a narration?

Bonus Question: Why did Charlotte say not to interrupt a narration?

Chapter 13—The Next Step

Narration Question #22: How to get the children to expand on their narration? Or do you just accept whatever they narrate, because it is "theirs"?

Narration Question #23: What's the difference between a narration question and a direct question on the content?

Narration Question #24: Why did Charlotte say that direct questions are a mistake?

Narration Question #25: Mason writes in Vol. 1, p. 233: "When the narration is over, there should be a little talk in which moral points are brought out, pictures shown to illustrate the lesson, or diagrams drawn on the blackboard." I'd like to know how we are to do this without encroaching upon the student's understanding of the text. How are we to bring out the moral points? I'm particularly interested in this as it pertains to literature and Bible.

Bonus Question: What kinds of "moral points" should we bring out in discussion questions?

Chapter 14—In Which We Talk More about When and How

Narration Question #26: Should narration be done immediately after a reading, or later in the day?

Narration Question #27: Does narration include asking questions to refresh memory when you continue reading a book another day?

Narration Question #28: I'm discouraged with narration and my 9-year-old. I'm using a classical education textbook and the sample narrations it gives don't resemble what my daughter narrates back to me. Hers are far less perfect. I am wondering how structured you think narration instructions should be? Is it too structured to ask a 9-year-old to narrate the story in no more than three sentences—and in one go? We often have to do a "rough draft" narration first, and then revise (as they are written narrations). I worry that the frustration is building and possibly spoiling a love for writing, no matter how patient I am with trying to help her develop her narration skills.

Bonus Question: Why did Charlotte do the pre-reading reviews?

Chapter 15—Magic Numbers

Narration Question #29: Do we require narrations of all books/subjects after age six? I seem to remember reading somewhere that certain subjects are just for enjoyment and they do not narrate them, but I cannot remember where I read that, or if it is true.

Narration Question #30: Should I make my kids narrate everything they (and I) read?

Narration Question #31: Should I vary the subjects daily in which narration is expected (for example: Monday-History, Tuesday-Literature, etc.) OR should I consistently have my children narrate from the same subject(s) each day, as in a written history narration is required after every history reading, etc.?

Narration Question #32: How many narrations should I require daily? Oral? Written? Both?

Bonus Question: How important is it to follow the grade level suggestions for narration requirements?

Chapter 16—Narration with Multiple Children

Narration Question #33: How do you do narration with multiple children? Does the youngest go first?

Narration Question #34: I have a 6th, 4th, and 3rd grader and sometimes it's a little tricky to make sure the first child doesn't narrate everything. I know it's been recommended to start with the youngest, then work your way up, but by the time the two younger students narrate, my oldest has been sitting there for 10 minutes before she has anything to add (if there is anything left).

Narration Question #35: If I do a read-aloud, should all of my children narrate (one after the other)?

Narration Question #36: How do you handle narration with multiple children at once? Or is it something you work on with children individually?

Narration Question #37: With many children to homeschool from 17 to 6, how do I incorporate narration? Daily with each? Different types? Some are working by themselves and others as a group with me. I just get overwhelmed with the idea and feel like it'll take a lot of time, so I don't do it much although I really want to.

Bonus Question: I know that narration helps cement the material in my student's mind, but are there any other benefits to doing narration?

Chapter 17—Beginning with Younger Children

Narration Question #38: In the *Learning and Living* DVD series you mention that narration should not be required of a child younger than six, if I remember correctly, including an example of not trying to do so "secretly" when daddy comes home. What is the difference between narration and asking questions about what the child did during a day or about what he saw/did when he went places? Would Charlotte Mason ask younger children any questions at all?

Narration Question #39: How do we begin narration with younger kids when they are first starting?

Narration Question #40: With littles just learning to write, how do you handle it when they do not want to dictate any longer, but say, "Mom, help me to write 'X'." When that "X" is about 8 sentences long, far beyond their ability to write themselves without frustration?

Bonus Question: Is narration too hard for young children?

Chapter 18—Beginning with Older Children

Narration Question #41: In the Fall I will have a 4th and 1st grader. I am going to try to have my 4th grader be more independent and therefore she will be reading more subjects/books on her on and then narrating her books to me. However there will be an overlap of the books they both will hear. I know when you are starting out with narration in 1st grade, it is recommended to start with Aesop's Fables. Do I still need to do this or can I have him narrate some of the science books that I will be reading to him instead of the Fables?

Narration Question #42: How should I begin narration if I am starting with older children who have not done it from the beginning?

Narration Question #43: How would you begin with older students: middle and high school levels?

Narration Question #44: When starting with a middle-school student, what's the best way to begin? Do I start with oral narration and then move into written? Is it better to start with read-alouds or with books she is reading independently, or both?

Bonus Question: My child prefers listening to me read over reading for herself. Should I urge her toward independent reading or continue to read aloud to her?

Chapter 19—Written Narration: The Next Step in Composition

Narration Question #45: When and how should I make the transition to having my child do written narrations?

Narration Question #46: How does one properly correct a narration for errors—both written and oral?

Narration Question #47: Should I be correcting my child's written narrations?

Narration Question #48: How do we know what needs to be corrected for our children if we are not that great at writing?

Narration Question #49: Is there some kind of guide you recommend for the teacher to use to help our children improve upon their written narrations?

Narration Question #50: Do you recommend any specific resources to assist the student's writing of a narration?

Bonus Question: My child likes to tell me his narration and then go write it down. Is that okay?

Chapter 20—Raising the Bar

Narration Question #51: What are the characteristics of a good narration? Is it important that they have a clear beginning, middle and end of the story? Does it have to be in complete sentences? What other specifics would define a good narration?

Narration Question #52: Can you briefly outline what depth of narration we should expect at different ages? Specifically, how will an upper elementary narration differ from a middle school narration, and how will a middle school narration differ from a high school narration?

Narration Question #53: Can you give examples of narration prompts for middle and then high school so we see how they change with our children's developing critical thinking skills?

Narration Question #54: Examples of specific written narration prompts for older kids would be beneficial. That transition time from tell me all you know to compare and contrast, etc. seems to be a sticking point with many.

Narration Question #55: How do we come up with narration questions that are more than "tell back what you read," especially if you have not read the material thoroughly yourself? Instead of having a separate writing course, I've always wanted to study a certain form of writing and then apply it to the daily narrations for that week, but I'm not sure how to work that out practically.

Bonus Question: Are there other ways we can vary narration assignments besides asking for the four types of narration?

Chapter 21—On the Side

Narration Question #56: Is it acceptable for the child to have the book close by as they are writing? My 11-year-old son is always wanting the book beside him, saying that he wants to make sure he spells the names of characters correctly, or to check other spellings. He is a pretty honest child and I have seen no evidence of him copying passages from the book; I just fear the skill/act of narration is not at the same level if he is in any way re-reading passages alongside writing the narration. I have tried writing key character names, places, and such on a whiteboard for him, but he still prefers the book to be at his side.

Narration Question #57: With narration, is there a place for note-taking?

Bonus Question: What are the top four things to remember when doing a narration lesson?

Chapter 22—Narration in High School

Narration Question #58: Is narration enough for high school level studies?

Narration Question #59: How much written narration for high school students? How many times per week, per subject? How long? How detailed? If they do a written narration, say, once or twice a week in history, chemistry, government and they have narrated orally in between—should I be looking for a summary of the whole week's reading to put it in written form at that point? Or should it be "just" a detailed account of today's reading like the oral ones? I struggle with this one because I feel like the kids may need the act of writing and recalling periodically in order to cement the knowledge they've gained through the week.

Narration Question #60: I am comfortable with narration for Bible, literature, and history, but what do you recommend for an Apologia high school science course? I want to stick with narration (as we've done with Apologia General Science) because comprehension of the material has been better than it was in my pre-C.M. days. Still, I am struggling with mistrusting narration for a high school level science course.

Narration Question #61: I'm most interested in narration at the high school level. Would LOVE to see samples of students at various levels, both from narration "veterans" as well as beginners.

Narration Question #62: How do high school students learn to write the various forms of papers?

Bonus Question: How important is it that my student excel in composition?

Chapter 23—An Added Bonus

Narration Question #63: How do I keep up with or judge narrations of independent readers/older students when I haven't read everything first myself?

Narration Question #64: When I haven't read the chapter or topic, how do I engage and comment on the narration?

Narration Question #65: How do I comment on, ask questions, and encourage more in-depth thinking on a middle school/high school narration (where my child read the material independently), when I am not closely familiar with the reading material?

Narration Question #66: How do I grade a narration or encourage deeper thinking on the content (middle/high school years in particular), when I truly don't know the difference between what my child included versus excluded from the reading material? (And given that one of my children has a major habit of skim reading.)

Narration Question #67: Should I be using narration when I have not actually read the material personally? Should I use narration, but use it alongside other methods such as assigning additional non-narrated materials/readings or a workbook/test sheet?

Section 3
More Narration Tips

Chapter 24
Do Not Bury Yourself in the Book

Charlotte Mason gave many practical tips to her teachers: some Do's and some Do Not's. In this chapter let's take a look at one of her Do Not's—a practical tip that will give us freedom to enjoy and encourage our children in their narrations.

"Do not bury yourself in the book while the children are reading aloud. Give your full attention to the reading, then when the time for narration comes receive what they tell you with your whole mind."

This guideline brings to mind a mental picture of a wife trying to talk to her husband while he has his nose buried in a newspaper . . . or a computer screen. It can be discouraging to feel that you are receiving only partial attention from your listener. He may be focused on your words, but something about that lack of eye contact tends to dampen your enthusiasm for sharing.

Charlotte reminded us that the same holds true for our children as they are reading aloud and narrating. Keep in mind that Charlotte was instructing teachers who would be working in a classroom setting. So our situation may be a bit different when it comes to the reading aloud part. Often, we sit beside the children and share the book as they read aloud. But in those situations where the children are facing us and reading aloud, we need to be careful that we are giving them our full attention. Don't use that time for checking e-mail or writing your grocery list.

When our children are narrating, especially, we need to give them our full attention, not bury our heads in the book to see what they are missing as they retell the passage. In fact, we will probably get better narrations if we make an effort to encourage our children with our full attention and facial expressions while they are working.

To make this Do Not even more practical, here are some specific things to think about and practice. Think of them as the teacher's responsibility during narration. The child's responsibility is to tell in full; the teacher's responsibility is to

- Make eye contact.
- Be aware of what your face is "saying."
- Listen eagerly with an attitude of a learner.
- Validate what the child remembered correctly.
- Mentally note any parts that might need clarification and include them in discussion questions after the narration.
- Share how your child's narration helped you learn something or brought you enjoyment.
- Recognize the work involved in a good narration and encourage your child toward continuing to improve that skill.

Some of you are way ahead of me here and thinking, *How am I going to make sure my child isn't forgetting anything or is getting the names correct or is telling the events in the right sequence if I don't follow along in the book?* It's a great question, and I think it shows more of Charlotte's genius in her methods. You see, she always encouraged the teachers to continue learning themselves. She thought no one was too old to form a new habit—especially the habit of attention.

Listening to a narration with full attention will rely on our giving full attention to the reading too, just as we expect our children to do. We will need to turn the full gaze of our mind's eye upon the material as we are reading. We will need to soak up the narrative in the book just as much as our children do.

In return, we will gain a sympathy of spirit with our children as we share the same experiences in the same living books. We will increase that heart-to-heart relationship we have with fellow learners who are walking the same path that we are. All the better that those fellow learners will be our children.

And we will keep our minds from becoming stagnant and weak. One of the benefits of homeschooling is that we can learn right alongside our children, and this Do Not is a perfect example of that bonus.

So get your head out of the book. Use your mind to learn along with your children, and use your face to encourage their efforts. Both of you will benefit from this Do Not.

*"Do not bury yourself in the book while the children are reading aloud. Give your full attention to the reading, then when the time for narration comes receive what they tell you with your whole mind. They will tell it all the better to someone who is listening and who is not consulting a book" (*The Story of Charlotte Mason*, pp. 150, 151).*

Chapter 25
Relating and Rambling

Mom took a deep breath and began to read aloud:

I wonder how many of my readers have ever sat upon an ottoman. If you have, you know that it . . .

"What's an ottoman, Mom?" six-year-old Stacy interrupted.

"If you listen, it will explain . . . " Mom began.

"It sounds like a super hero: Otto-Man!" eight-year-old Nathan chimed in with a grin.

"I wonder what his super power would be?" Stacy added. "Maybe he would . . . "

"Let's get back to the story and see what an ottoman really is," directed Mom, and she picked up where she had left off.

. . . you know that it is a soft, round, tufted stool, comfortable for resting your feet, especially a father's feet after a long day spent hard at work. . . .

"Dad doesn't put his feet up after he gets home from work," mentioned Nathan.

"It sounds something like a footstool," said Stacy. "Why don't they just say 'footstool'?"

"What time is Dad getting home tonight, anyway?" asked Nathan.

Mom plowed ahead.

. . . I fancy you may wonder how it got such a funny name. Well, when . . .

"I didn't say it was a funny name," explained Stacy. "I just wondered why they didn't use the name 'footstool.' After all, that's what it is, and . . . "

Mom tried to redirect focus.

. . . when the furniture maker began making this new kind of footstool . . .

"There you go," interjected Nathan. "They just said it was a footstool."

"Oh, good," replied Stacy. "But I still wonder why they didn't just say that in the first place. Why did they call it an ottoman?"

"You are about to find out," sighed Mother, "if you will just listen."

. . . he called it an "ottoman" because its shape reminded him of the round hats worn by officials in the Ottoman Empire. . . .

"Sailors wear round hats too," added Stacy.

Mom shut the book.

Charlotte Mason told us that Education is the Science of Relations. We want our children to form personal relations and to make mental connections with what they are hearing or reading.

In the scenario above, were Stacy and Nathan forming relations? Yes. Their minds were busy thinking of what else in their experience was connected to what they were hearing. They were curious and they were mentally interacting with the narrative.

But they were also frustrating their mother and hindering the story. Why? Because they were allowing their thoughts to ramble.

Charlotte described it this way:

"You talk to a child about glass—you wish to provoke a proper curiousity as to how glass is made, and what are its uses. Not a bit of it; he wanders off to Cinderella's glass slipper; then he tells you about his *godmother who gave him a boat; then about the ship in which Uncle Harry*

went to America; then he wonders why you do not wear spectacles, leaving you to guess that Uncle Harry does so. But the child's ramblings are not whimsical; they follow a law, the law of association of ideas, by which any idea presented to the mind recalls some other idea which has been at any time associated with it—as glass, and Cinderella's slipper; and that, again some idea associated with it. Now this law of association of ideas is a good servant and a bad master" (Vol. 1, p. 138).

The difference between helpful relating and distracting rambling is in whether we allow the law of association to be a servant or a master.

Directing the Thoughts

As a servant, the law of association will help us recall what we need to remember when we need it. But as a master, the law of association will make our home schools a tiring tug-of-war.

Charlotte recognized that fact:

"Here is the secret of the weariness of the home schoolroom—the children are thinking all the time about something else than their lessons; or rather, they are at the mercy of the thousand fancies that flit through their brains, each in the train of the last" (Vol. 1, p. 139).

We must help our children learn to give direction to these trains of thought. A vigorous effort of will should enable them to turn the gaze of their mind's eye away from those flitting fancies and onto the lesson at hand. And as they exercise their mental "muscles" in this way, they will subdue the law of association and make it their servant, rather than their master.

As with any muscle-strengthening exercise, it will take effort. It will take time. It will take patience. But we owe it to our children to help them stop their rambling and learn to direct their thoughts.

"Where is the harm? In this: not merely that the children are wasting time, though that is a pity; but that they are forming a desultory habit of mind, and reducing their own capacity for mental effort" (Vol. 1, p. 139).

So how do you go about helping your child direct his thoughts and get control over the distracting rambling? Here are a few ideas.

- During a neutral time—not in the middle of a lesson—mention that commenting in the middle of the reading is like interrupting. He is interrupting the author. Briefly explain that you want to help him learn good listening manners, whether in conversation or in school work.

- Use the same technique Charlotte described for reinforcing the habit of attention. Start short. Before you begin to read, remind the child about not interrupting. Explain that you will stop at times to allow him to add his comments, but he is not to blurt out those comments in between stops. Start with one or two paragraphs, then invite comments.

Gradually lengthen the reading time as your child progresses in this listening etiquette.

- Make sure your child is getting enough time between readings in order to process all of his relations and explore all of those trains of thought on his own. Charlotte did not schedule reading from the same book every day; she scheduled time between readings for the child to ruminate on what he had heard.

Chapter 26
Narration with Auditory and Speech Issues

The art of narrating—telling back what you know in your own words—can be a challenge for most every student. But for those who struggle with auditory processing or speech issues, narration can be even more challenging—for both student and parent.

Doubts can arise: Should I require him to narrate at all? Is he capable of this or am I asking him to do something he cannot do? Am I challenging or frustrating my child?

While each parent knows his or her child best, I can share what my experience has been. My youngest is fifteen, but it has only been in the past few years that I've required a narration from her. She has autism and developmental delays that affect her language skills, both auditory and speech. So I waited until she was able to use sentences in spontaneous conversation around the house first. I figured if she wasn't able to compose a sentence in her own words in an informal setting, she shouldn't be pressured to do so in a lesson setting.

We've certainly had our ups and downs, but I wanted to share with you what has been working well lately. Maybe it will give you some ideas for your own situations.

Steps in Narration with Delayed Language Skills

Here are the steps I've been using when we read and narrate from a book.

1. Choose a short story; only a few paragraphs. We have worked up to a page or two for history selections, but for Bible and science, we are still keeping it at a few paragraphs.
   Ideally, the selection will contain a complete idea or event even when it is broken into sections. For example, we recently read about how Samoset brought Squanto to help the Pilgrims. That large event, which historically covered several days or weeks, we broke into smaller events for the readings. The first reading was about Samoset's coming; the second reading was about his telling them he had a friend named Squanto, whom he would bring to help them. The third reading was about Squanto's coming; the fourth reading was about Squanto's showing the Pilgrims how to plant corn with little fish in the soil.
   Short selections are especially crucial to help our language-strugglers gain confidence and practice the habit of full attention.

2. Show a picture or object that illustrates some aspect of what you will be reading about. If there is a picture in the book, I'll show it to her and we'll discuss what we see. I try to use this exercise to build a sense of assured anticipation but not give spoilers. If there isn't a picture in the book, I'll find one on the Internet or use simple objects around the house.
   We recently read a poem about four children standing on the edge of the pond, looking at four waterlilies. So I found a photo on the Internet of four waterlilies floating in some water. It took about two minutes to find it. I drug the image onto my desktop so it would be right

there when I was ready for it. Double-click to open it, and we're off and running with no distractions or delays while I try to find it again in my browser. (This little tip can prevent a lot of frustration. Don't ask me how I know.)

Today we were going to read about an oak tree that shed its leaves and covered some flowers for the winter. So before we read, we went outside to look at a tree in the front yard that had shed its leaves on the flowers below it. We talked about how the leaves made a blanket to keep the flowers from freezing, and she made a relation with other objects that freeze that she is familiar with.

In this step I'm trying to prime the pump and use her stronger visual skills to get her started. Once she has a schema, a mental picture of the context, of what she will be hearing, we're ready to move on.

3. Write on the white board two or three key words from the selection. Last week, for example, we read the Bible account of Jesus' clearing the temple and overturning the money-changers' tables. I picked the words "Jesus," "temple," and "greedy people," because I knew she understood the concept of "greedy."

   After we look at the picture, I have her read the key words aloud to me and I tell her that those words will be in the story. She should listen for/look for them and include them in her narration too.

4. Read the selection. Read at the pace that works best for the child, but be careful not to sacrifice inflection and enunciation. You can read slowly and still read expressively. Then again, be careful not to go overboard and get melodramatic, overdoing all the emotions in the story. Try to read as you would to any other student, just slower as needed.

5. Ask the student to tell the story, being sure to use all the key words on the board. Since my daughter has slow processing, especially when trying to use language, I have a spiral notebook in which I write each sentence after she gives it. It seems that the extra time it takes for me to write gives her more processing time to come up with another sentence. If, on the other hand, I simply sit and look at her and listen while she's trying to narrate, she feels pressured to come up with the next sentence more quickly and usually shuts down. But if I nod and smile at her first sentence, then shift my gaze to the notebook, and slowly and carefully write it, she doesn't feel as "put on the spot" and can usually come up with another sentence or two while I'm busy writing the first one. I consider a two- or three-sentence narration a victory!

Looking over those steps, it strikes me that they are very similar to the steps of a narration lesson that Charlotte Mason gave for all children. How nice that the framework is the same! We can simply adjust a bit here and there as each child needs.

It looks like the main adjustments I've made have been in the length of the selection we read; giving pre-reading visual context, even for familiar objects; looking away and giving extra time to compose each sentence without pressure; and the length of narration that I expect.

Chapter 20
A Whole World of Thought

Last week we went to a park with a pond amid lovely gardens. The path wanders around the pond and features several benches and bench swings on which you can rest and gaze out over the water. As we meandered down the path, we rounded the curve on the far end of the pond and caught sight of one lone duck sitting on top of the water.

As we watched, it stuck its head into the pond. I was prepared for "up tails all," but this duck didn't do that. It disappeared, completely underwater! A moment or two later it resurfaced and sat there as before. I was intrigued and paused on the path to see what it would do next. Sure enough, in a few minutes it dove under the water again, straight down, stayed out of sight for a bit, then eventually reappeared.

I'd never seen anything like it. Happily, my friend Karen was with me and told me this behavior was normal for this kind of duck: it was a diving duck.

It was fascinating to think about what was happening under that water. We knew the duck was swimming and feeding under there—looking for aquatic plants and chasing fish for its dinner—but we couldn't see any of that. All we could see was the dive and the resurfacing.

Between the dive and the resurfacing lies a whole world of activity.

The same is true for narration.

Narration Under the Surface

Essex Cholmondley, a friend and biographer of Charlotte Mason, wisely observed:

> "Between attention and expression lies a whole world of thought."

On the surface, narration seems simple. Sometimes it seems almost too simple. It's not unusual for a homeschool mom to pull me aside at a convention and confide, "We switched to a Charlotte Mason approach last year and we're enjoying it so much. But there are days when I think we are enjoying it too much; that reading and narrating is too simple. Surely we must be missing something."

That's when I have the pleasure of confirming that methods can be simple yet effective. Even though narration may look simple on the surface, underneath it all, the students are busy in a world of thought.

Because we are using quality living books, that world of thought is a rich one. They are being given worthy thoughts and well-told tales with ideas worth thinking about.

It is an unhurried world where ideas are planted a bit at a time with space in between. And in that spacing they have time to think, which is a precious place to live.

It is a personal world, for it gives each student the freedom to think individually rather than as one of a crowd and offers him the prize of knowledge as his own possession.

It is a wide world, for we read on a variety of topics and from a variety of authors. The students can explore far and wide with generous boundaries in their thoughts.

We probably will not see that mental exploring as it happens. Most likely we cannot watch the feasting as it occurs on the wonderful ideas spread for the student, because that activity happens in this world we have described—a world of thought. A world we cannot see.

But we can see the results of what is happening under the surface. Just as with the diving duck, my friend and I could see that it was healthy, hardy, and whole because of its activity under the water, so we can see the results of our students' explorations in that rich, wide, unhurried, personal world of thought. The results are seen in their words, in their attitudes, in their choices, in their habits. The results are seen in who they are becoming.

On the surface we may see only a child listening and narrating, but rest assured that "between attention and expression lies a whole world of thought."